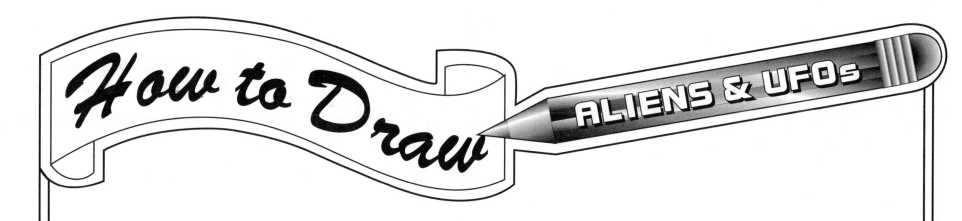

How to Draw ALIENS & UFOs

Illustrated by Jael

Copyright © 1997 Kidsbooks Inc.
3535 West Peterson Avenue
Chicago, IL 60659

Visit us at www.kidsbooks.com
Volume discounts available for group purchases.

INTRODUCTION

This book will show you how to draw lots of different aliens and UFOs. Some are more difficult than others, but if you follow along, step-by-step, you'll soon be able to draw all the figures in this book. Then, by using these methods and (most importantly!) your imagination, you'll soon be able to create your own aliens and UFOs.

The most basic and commonly used shape is the oval. There are many variations of ovals—some are small and round, others are long and flat, and many are in-between. Often a free-form oval, like the ones pictured below, is used.

Each alien and UFO drawing in this book begins with a line or stick figure. This establishes the basic body position of the subject. Then, different kinds of ovals and other shapes are added over the line figure to round out the body, limbs, and other sections.

Note: When forming the limbs of most aliens, the basic shapes usually overlap.

Some basic oval shapes:

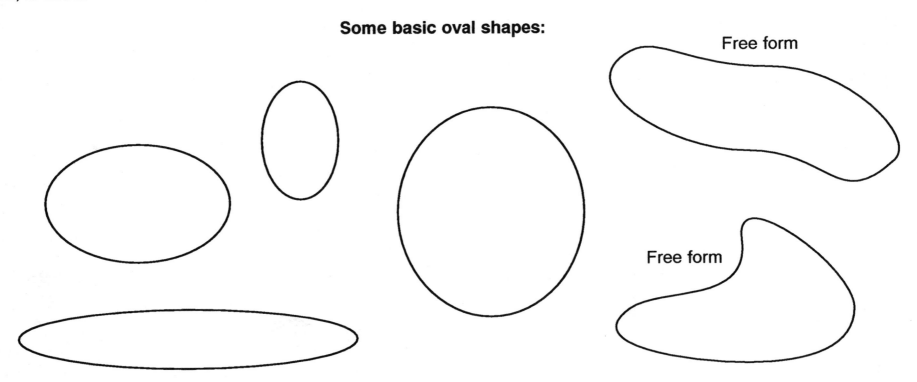

Free form

Free form

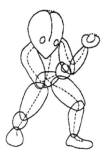
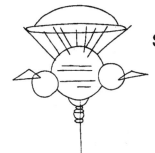

SUPPLIES

SOFT PENCILS (#2 OR SOFTER)
DRAWING PAD
SOFT ERASER
COLORED PENCILS,
MARKERS, OR CRAYONS

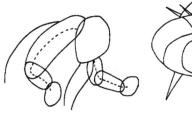
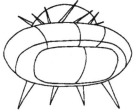

HELPFUL HINTS

1. In the first two steps you will create a solid foundation of the figure—much like a builder who must first construct a foundation before building the rest of the house. Next comes the fun part—creating the smooth, clean outline drawing of the alien or UFO, and adding all the finishing touches—details, shading, and color. Following the first two steps carefully will make the final steps easier.

2. **Always keep your pencil lines light and soft**. These "guidelines" will be easier to erase when you no longer need them.

3. Don't be afraid to erase. It usually takes a lot of drawing and erasing before you will be satisfied with the way your drawing looks.

4. Add details and all the finishing touches after you have blended and refined all the shapes and your drawing is complete.

5. Remember: **Practice Makes Perfect.** Don't be discouraged if you can't get the hang of it right away. Just keep drawing and erasing until you do.

Adding the finishing touches is the fun part of any drawing. Add your own details, shading, or colors. Feel free to change one or more features. What you see here and on the following pages is simply a guide to help you get started.

HOW TO START

1. Begin by drawing a stick figure like the one on this page. This will give the figure a basic pose. It also helps make the figure look like it's moving in one direction or another. The action and movement of a figure is called "gesture."

2. Add the oval shapes to the stick figure. Note that many of these ovals are not perfect. These are the basic guidelines that form the figure and create the foundation. **REMEMBER TO KEEP YOUR LINES LIGHTLY DRAWN.**

3. Carefully draw the parts of the figure within the oval guidelines. When you are satisfied with your drawing, erase the guidelines, including the stick figure. Blend the various shapes and forms so that your drawing has a smooth, flowing look.

Note: The dotted lines show what can be erased as you go along.

4. & 5. Complete and refine facial features, limbs, clothing, and any special effects. Add all the other details and finishing touches to complete your drawing. Color your finished alien or UFO with your favorite colors or, for a more dramatic effect, outline them with a thick, black marker.

Use your imagination and create different objects and backgrounds to enhance your drawings. When you have drawn some or all of the aliens and UFOs in this book, and are comfortable with your drawing technique, start creating your own.

Most of all, **HAVE FUN!**

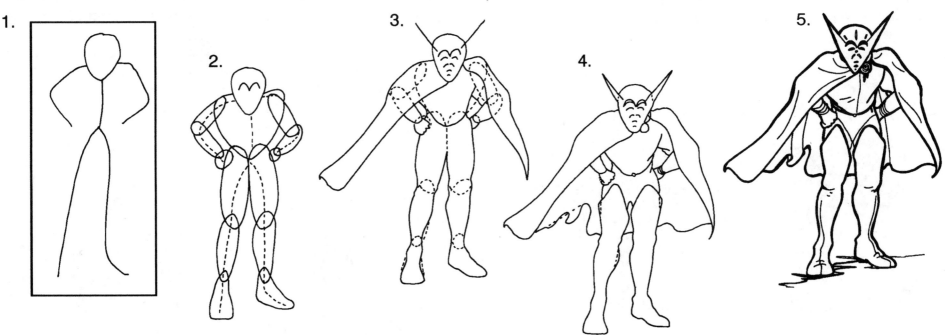

BLASTO

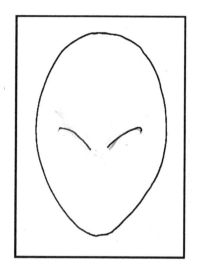

1. Draw a simple oval in the shape of a head. Remember to draw it lightly. In the center, add two slightly curved lines.

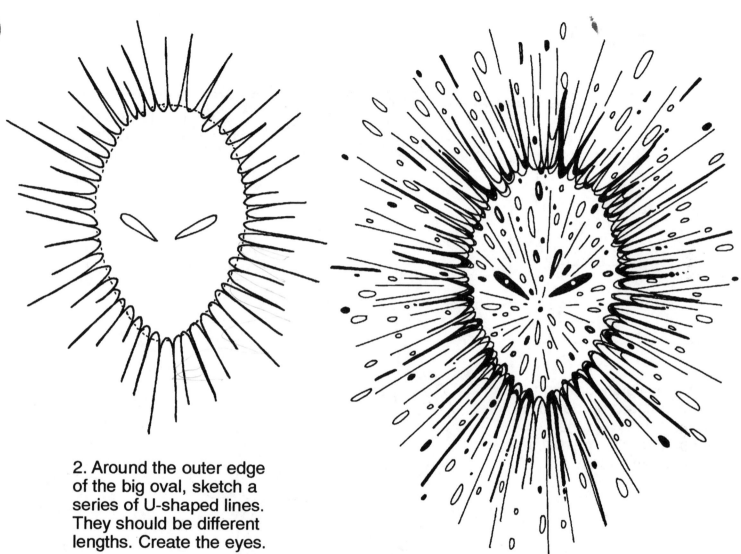

2. Around the outer edge of the big oval, sketch a series of U-shaped lines. They should be different lengths. Create the eyes.

3. Starting at the center, draw lots of straight lines and small ovals. Fill some of the ovals in with a felt-tip pen. Keep drawing them until they burst off your page!

HEELIO

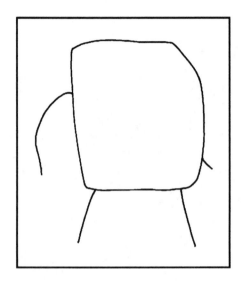

1. & 2.
Begin by lightly drawing the line figure of the box shape. Then add the ovals and other guideline shapes, as shown.

Remember: Always keep your pencil lines light and soft, so the guidelines will be easier to erase when you no longer need them.

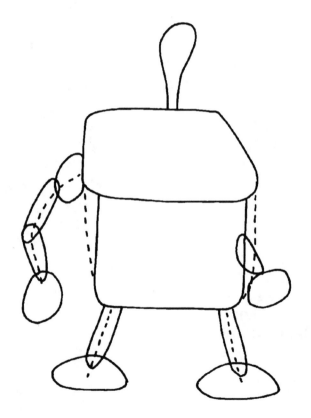

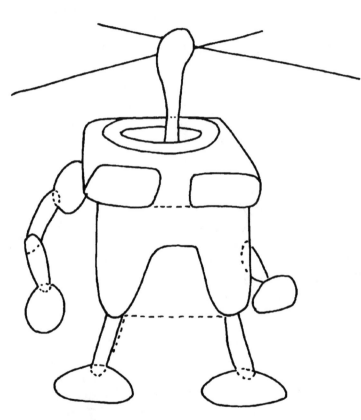

3. Add the other guideline shapes to the top section, including lines for the rotor blades. Define the upper section of the legs.

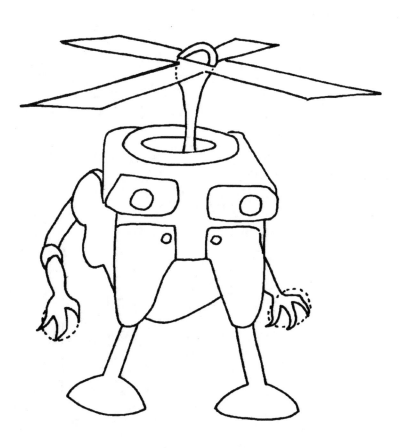

4. Draw the claws and the rotor blades. Continue to add lines and shapes to the main box figure. Erase any unneeded guidelines as you go along.

5. Complete your drawing by adding lots of details to Heelio. Add as many as you like. Curved lines between the rotor blades will make them appear to be spinning. When you're satisfied with your picture, outline it with a heavy, felt-tip pen.

GHAR DEYEN, THE GALACTIC MONITOR

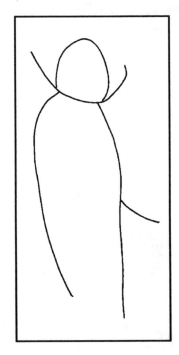

Hint: Draw these key steps carefully. Get the stick figure to gesture in the directions you want it to. By carefully adding the ovals over the stick figure, you have created a solid foundation. This will give your figure a more realistic look after you've completed the next steps.

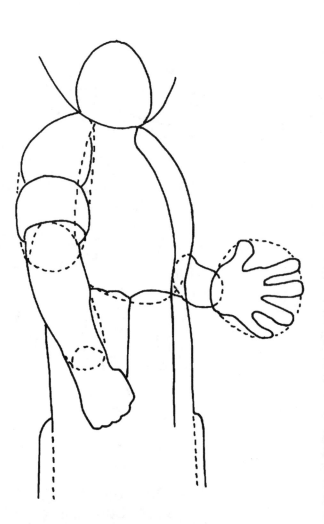

1. & 2. Start by sketching the basic line figure. Then add the ovals and other guideline shapes for the arms, hands, and body.

3. Start defining and shaping the arms and hands within the oval guidelines. Carefully draw fingers on the left hand. Erase the gesture lines as you go along.

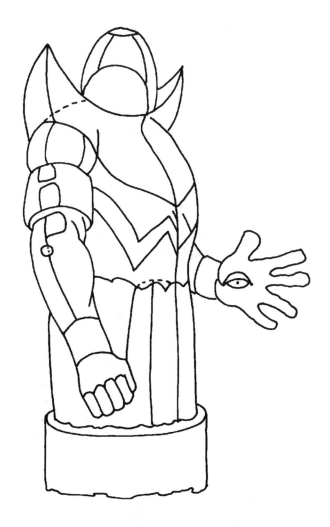

4. Add the shapes and lines to the arm, the collar, and the body suit. Draw fingers on the right hand and an eye on the left hand. Blend and refine all the shapes into a smooth outline of this alien.

5. For the finishing touches, add details to Galactic Monitor's bodysuit and head. Ghar Deyen's watchful eye never closes. No one has been able to pass through the solar gateway he guards...yet.

KOPPY

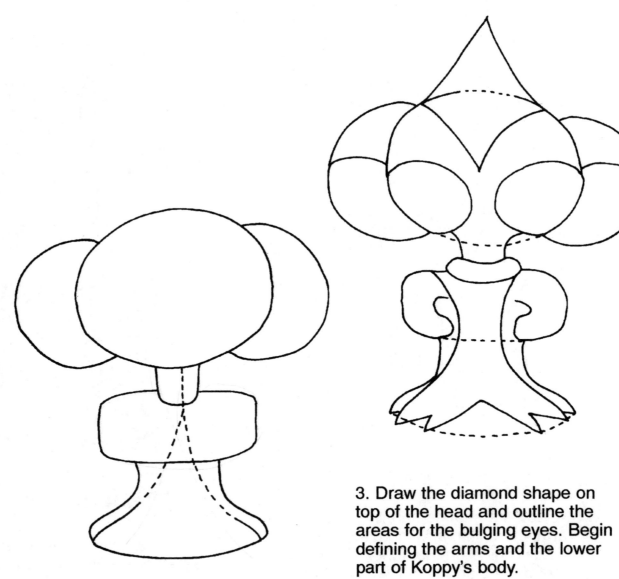

1. & 2. Begin by lightly sketching a large oval stick figure. Add the two half-ovals on either side of the main one to complete the guide-lines for the head. Then draw the simple shapes for the alien's body.

3. Draw the diamond shape on top of the head and outline the areas for the bulging eyes. Begin defining the arms and the lower part of Koppy's body.

4. Keep working on the body. Carefully draw Koppy's two fingers that serve as arms, and his six pointy toes that serve as feet. Refine the diamond shape and begin drawing the squiggly vertical lines on the eyes. Add the nose and the mouth.

5. Finish the eyes. Add lots of details and color to complete your alien drawing. Koppy is a robozoid who directs space traffic. His eyes flash colors for "Stop" and "Go."

ALIEN SPACE BLASTER

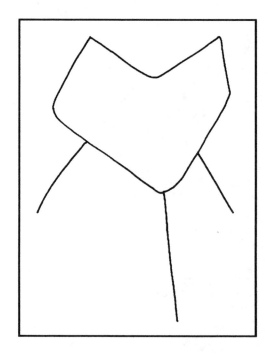

1. Lightly sketch the craft's shape and the three lines on the bottom.

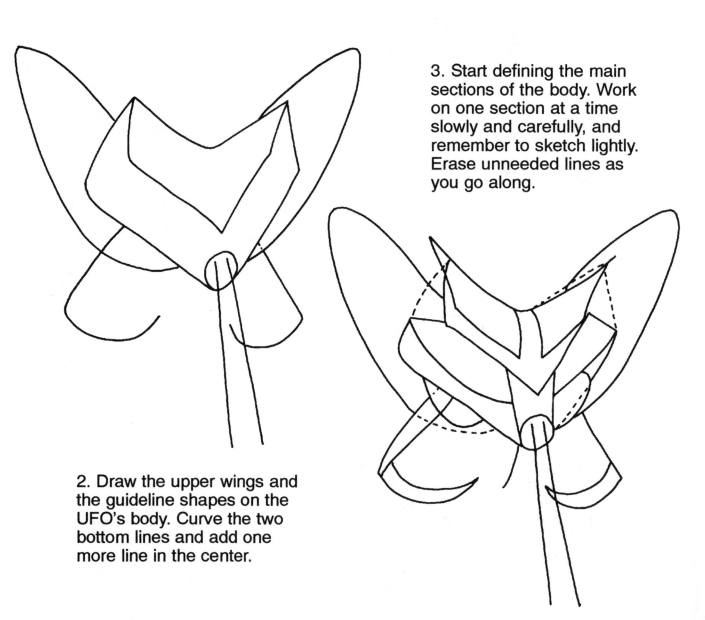

2. Draw the upper wings and the guideline shapes on the UFO's body. Curve the two bottom lines and add one more line in the center.

3. Start defining the main sections of the body. Work on one section at a time slowly and carefully, and remember to sketch lightly. Erase unneeded lines as you go along.

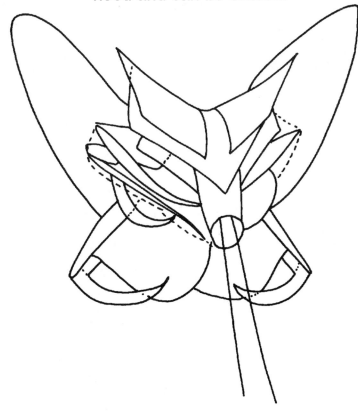

Note: The dotted lines are guidelines you no longer need and can be erased.

4. Keep refining the main part of the craft. Then complete the lower section of Space Blaster.

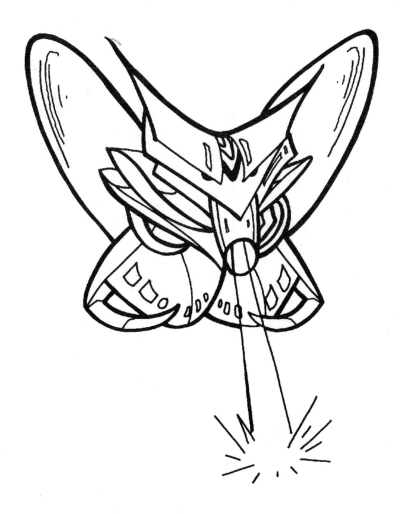

5. Add all the details that will give your drawing a finished look.

THE NASTIES

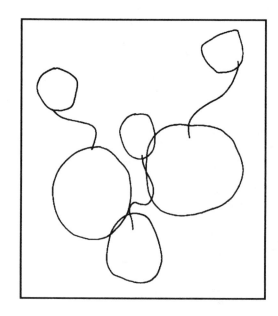

1. Draw three large ovals, curved lines, and three small ovals in that order. These Nasties are hatching out of rotten eggs found in space volcanoes.

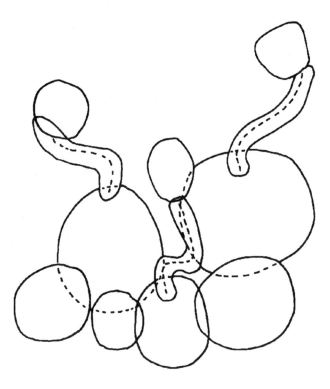

2. Create the snakelike bodies and add three more overlapping ovals.

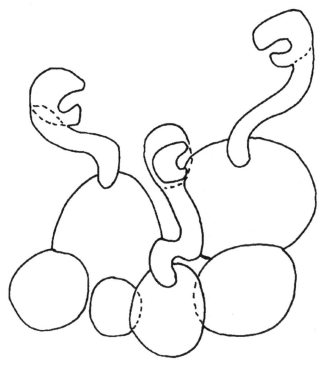

3. Erase any unneeded guidelines and define the outlines of the three mouths.

4. Draw the Nasties' sharp, curved teeth and add features to their heads as shown. Add as many unhatched eggs as you like and begin adding details.

5. Continue to add spots on the eggs and other details. The vertical squiggly lines represent the smelly odor of rotten eggs. When the Nasties are ready, color them with some nasty colors.

THE WASPIE

1. Draw the simple shapes as shown.

2. Create guidelines for the eyes on the small oval. Then start dividing the large oval into sections. Draw the guideline for the stem of the tentacles.

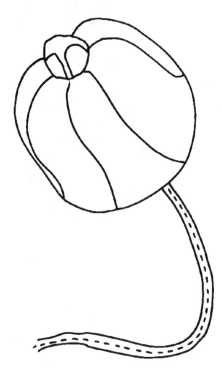

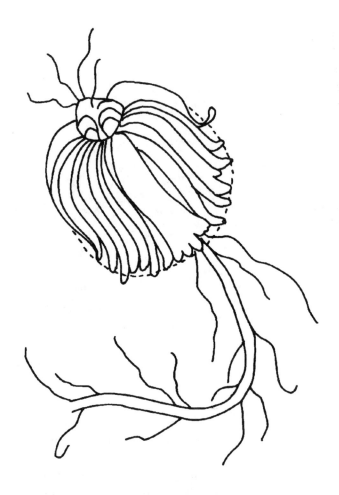

3. Begin defining the eyes. Continue to divide the main oval into smaller sections. Add a few crooked lines on the head and lots of them on the stem. Waspie stings with its sharply barbed tentacles. Erase unnecessary guidelines.

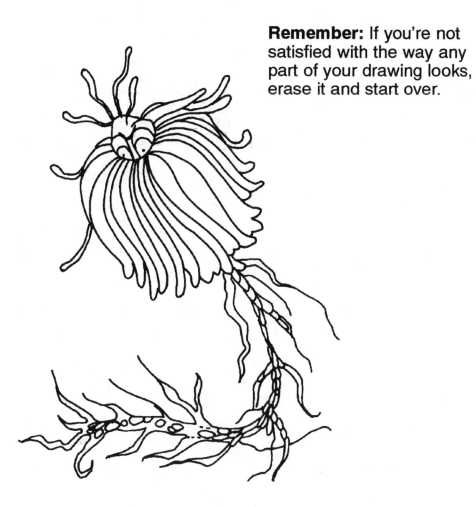

Remember: If you're not satisfied with the way any part of your drawing looks, erase it and start over.

4. Add two dots for the eyes and start creating tentacles. Take your time and draw as many as you wish.

5. Finish the barbed tentacles, and when Waspie is complete, color it with your favorite colors.

DRACC

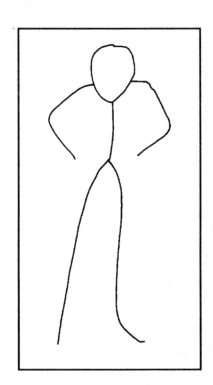

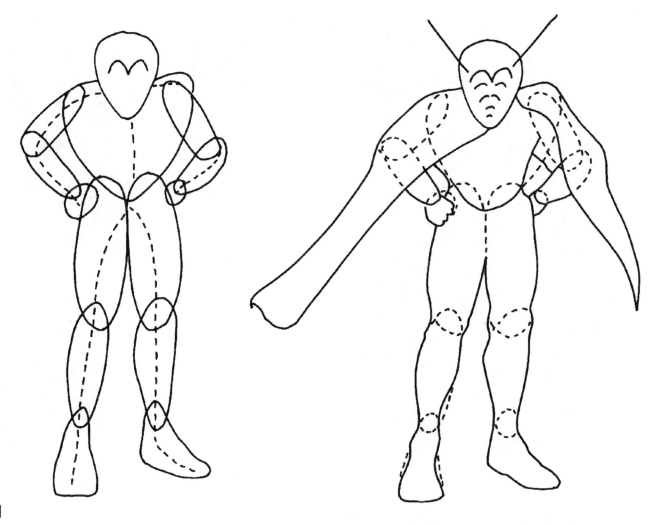

1. & 2.

Lightly draw the line figure and the oval guideline shapes. Be extra careful as you overlap all the ovals. Add a double arch on the helmet.

3. Add guidelines for the flowing cape. Then add the curved lines on the helmet and two guidelines for its horns. Begin blending the outline for Dracc's body.

18

4. Complete blending the body parts, erasing any guidelines you no longer need. Complete the helmet, cape, and boots, and start adding details. Create the arms before you add the cape. This will make the pose more realistic.

5. Finish Dracc by making his horned helmet sharp and pointed. Add all the finishing touches. Color Dracc or outline the drawing with a felt-tip pen.

THE ANDROMEDA BLOB

1. & 2.
Draw a free-form shape and
two small ovals. Add a
straight line on one side and
a curved line on the other.
Erase any unnecessary lines.

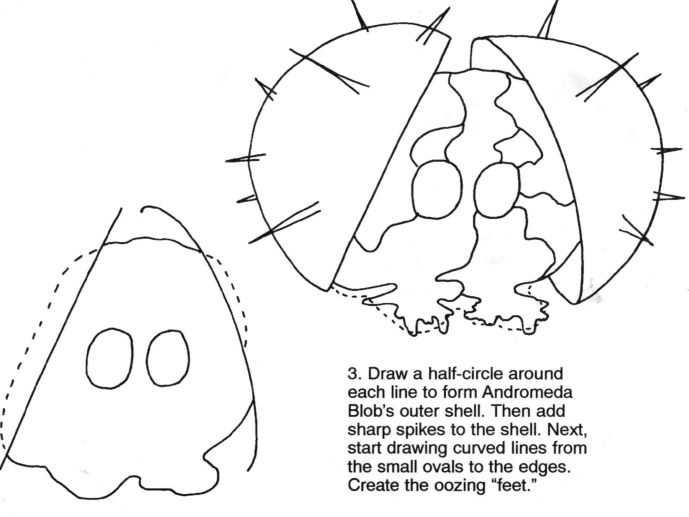

3. Draw a half-circle around
each line to form Andromeda
Blob's outer shell. Then add
sharp spikes to the shell. Next,
start drawing curved lines from
the small ovals to the edges.
Create the oozing "feet."

Remember: If at any point you're not satisfied with your drawing, erase and start again.

5. Add details to the shell and dark shading to the center section. When your Blob is finished, outline it with a heavy felt-tip pen.

4. Add two small circles within the ovals to help the Blob see where it's oozing. Keep adding lines to the center section to form a pattern. Feel free to create any pattern you wish, as long as it's creepy!

ELLOSYX

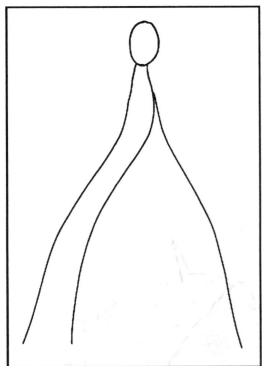

1. & 2.
Draw the stick figure with long, flowing guidelines and add the simple shapes as shown.

3. Shape the ear and add the other features to Ellosyx's head. Then fill in the shapes for the lower body and front feet. Ellosyx is a very gentle alien, who, in spite of large feet, can step lightly through a field of blossoms.

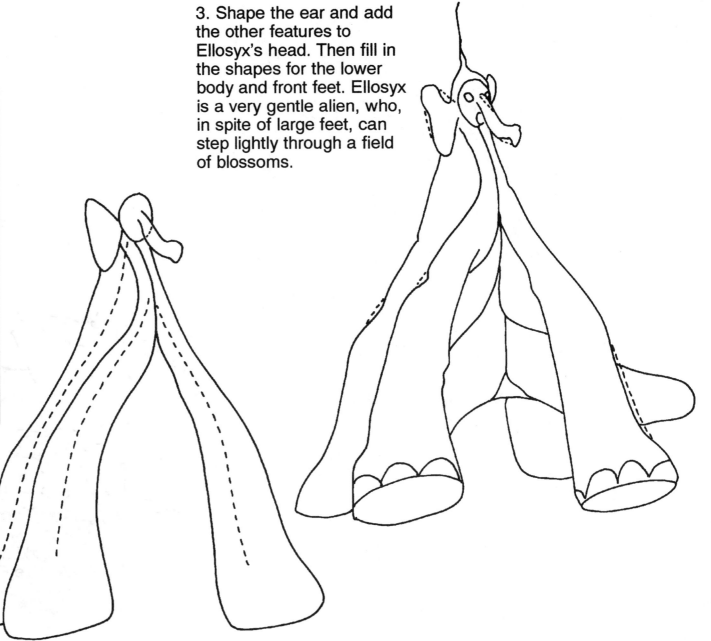

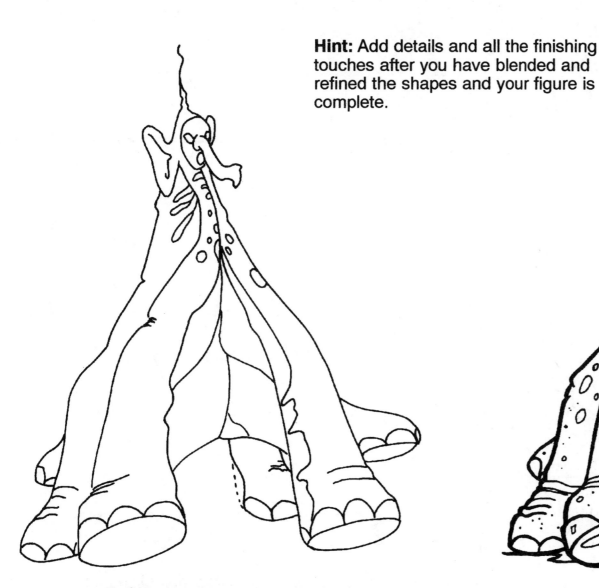

Hint: Add details and all the finishing touches after you have blended and refined the shapes and your figure is complete.

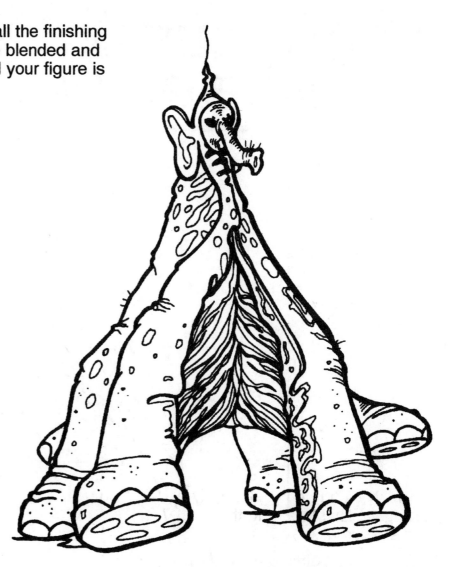

4. Refine the ear, trunk, and other facial features. Then create the other four feet and start adding texture and details to the body.

5. Add texture and details to give Ellosyx your own personal touch.

23

FUSCIA, QUEEN OF SPACE GEMS

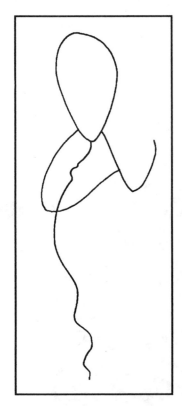

1. & 2.
Begin with the lightly drawn gesturing stick figure. Then add the free-form ovals, a diagonal line, and a curved guideline as shown.

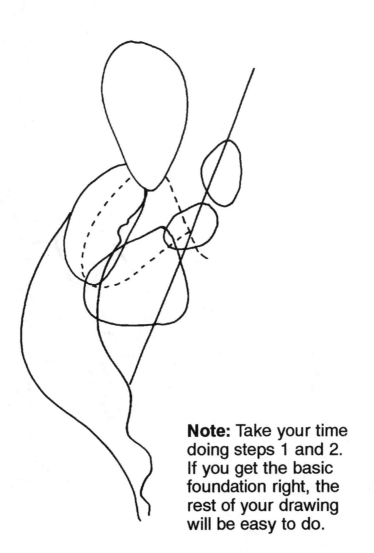

Note: Take your time doing steps 1 and 2. If you get the basic foundation right, the rest of your drawing will be easy to do.

3. Draw guidelines for Fuscia's cape, sleeves, hands, and facial features. Create her gem-making staff. Erase unneeded guidelines as you go along.

4. Add more lines to her face, creating Fuscia's mouth, and begin adding a pattern of lines on her head. Draw her hood, then slowly and carefully refine her cape, sleeve, and hands. Bring the curved lines of her cape to a point near the bottom of your page and connect them to a precious gem.

5. Complete the pattern on the head. Add all the details, shading, and final touches that will give your picture a finished look. If you choose to color Fuscia, she should really glow and sparkle.

AURORA, DANCER OF SOLAR WINDS

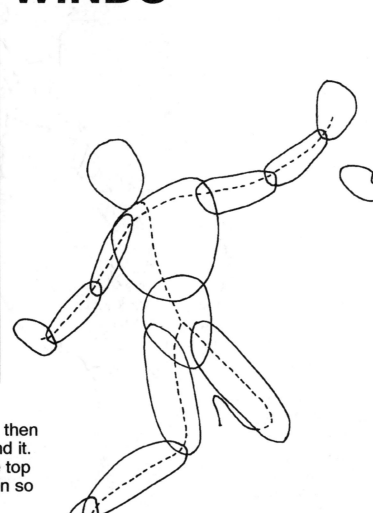

1. & 2.
Draw the gesturing stick figure, then add the guideline shapes around it. It's usually easier to start at the top and work down, especially when so many of the ovals overlap.

3. Smooth out the body, then add more guideline shapes to Aurora's head. Blend all the shapes into a refined body outline. Add the outline of the cape.

Hint: What you see here is only one example of what the finishing touches can look like. Always feel free to use your imagination when completing an imaginary figure. Add details as you wish.

4. Draw the facial features and begin adding overlapping scales to the torso. Start at the top row and work down. Define the fingers and add rows of curved lines on Aurora's arms and legs, as shown.

5. Continue adding lines on Aurora's arms and legs, and scales on the body. Finish the face and add all the details that will complete your picture.

GALACTIC BATTLE STATION

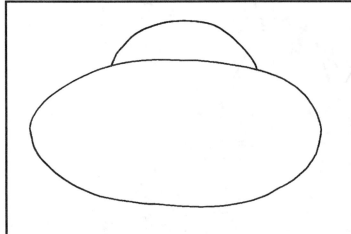

1. & 2. Draw a huge oval with a semi-circle on top. Add a rectangle with rounded corners within the large oval. Then draw four short guidelines on the bottom of the craft.

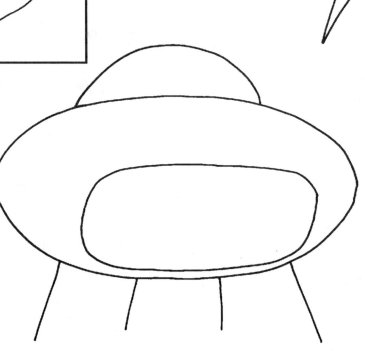

3. Lightly sketch the shapes for the different sections. Add a series of spikes on the top section and complete the four on the bottom.

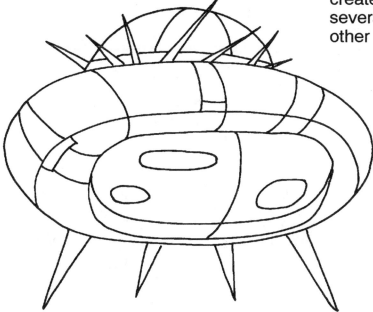

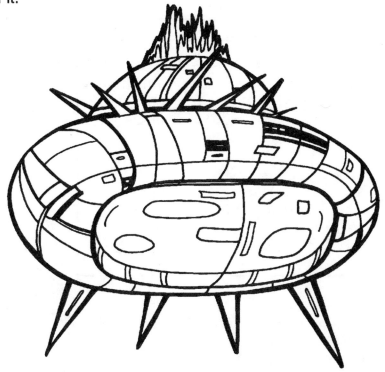

Hint: Always use your imagination when adding details. It's also fun to create a scene in deep space with several UFOs, space stations, and other alien craft in it.

4. Continue adding sections to the Battle Station. Take it one section at a time and, as you complete each section, erase any unnecessary guidelines. This station has many ovals, but you don't have to be too precise. Add as many sections and windows as you like.

5. Keep adding lots of sections, windows, hatches, and other details to the Battle Station until you are satisfied with the way it looks. Then outline it with a heavy felt-tip pen.

MITZEE,
THE COSMIC BUG

Remember: If you're not satisfied with the way any part of your drawing looks, erase it and start again.

1. & 2.
Draw the basic stick figure, then the overlapping guideline shapes. Add a curved line for the wing and lines for the antennae.

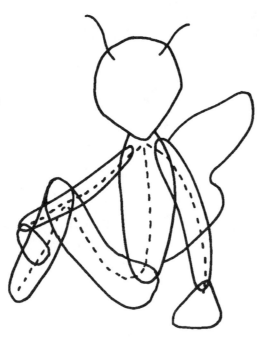

3. Complete the antennae and add ovals for the eyes. Shape the limbs and hands, and begin adding the petals of the alien flower. Add the second wing.

4. Refine the face and body, erasing lines you no longer need. Add more petals and begin making them jagged.

5. Darken this alien's eyes and add details to its body and wings. Finish your drawing by outlining it with a magic marker. This will make it look bold and strong.

GALAXIA

1. Lightly draw the gesturing stick figure. Galaxia is a shadowy, spooky form in the night sky.

2. Sketch the outline of the body around the stick figure, ending each limb with uneven, pointy, thornlike shapes.

3. To make a really fun and scary picture, use white chalk to draw the creature on black paper.

BUBBLOW

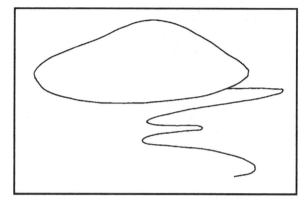

1. & 2.
Draw the basic figure as shown. Then add tiny ovals and circles around the edges of the big oval. The circles on top are soapy bubbles, and the ovals on the bottom are tiny feet. Note the oval for the eye and the shape of the open mouth.

3. Carefully form Bubblow's feet, erasing guidelines as you go along. Define the eye and be sure to draw lots of soap bubbles. Draw the soapy trail Bubblow leaves behind. This alien is a Soap-apede and its job is to gobble up space pollution.

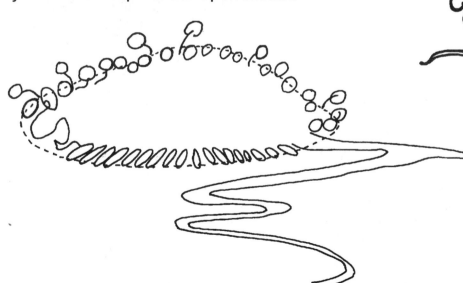

4. Outline the feet and most of the bubbles with a felt-tip pen. What colors should the bubbles be?

SULPHURO

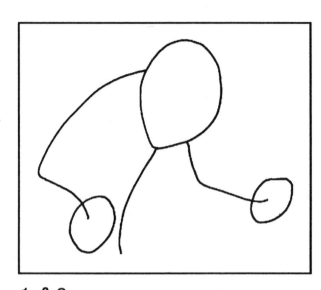

1. & 2.
Draw the gesturing stick figure and the overlapping ovals.

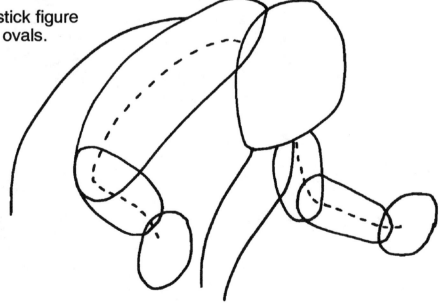

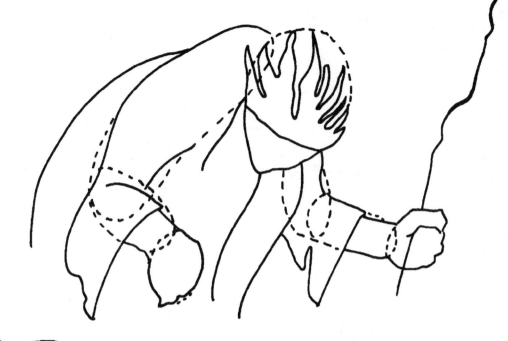

3. Create the flaming hair and the sleeves of Sulphuro's robe. Add a guideline for his staff. Begin to carve out the shapes for hands.

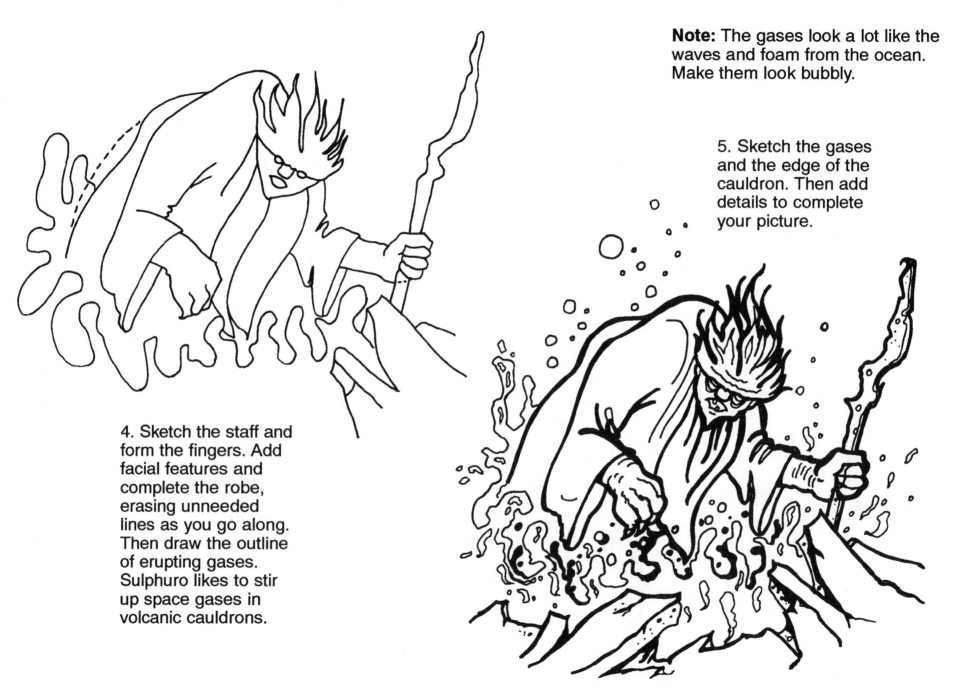

Note: The gases look a lot like the waves and foam from the ocean. Make them look bubbly.

5. Sketch the gases and the edge of the cauldron. Then add details to complete your picture.

4. Sketch the staff and form the fingers. Add facial features and complete the robe, erasing unneeded lines as you go along. Then draw the outline of erupting gases. Sulphuro likes to stir up space gases in volcanic cauldrons.

ELECTRO

1. & 2.
Starting with the oval head, draw the line figure. Carefully add overlapping ovals. Start with the torso, then add one limb at a time.

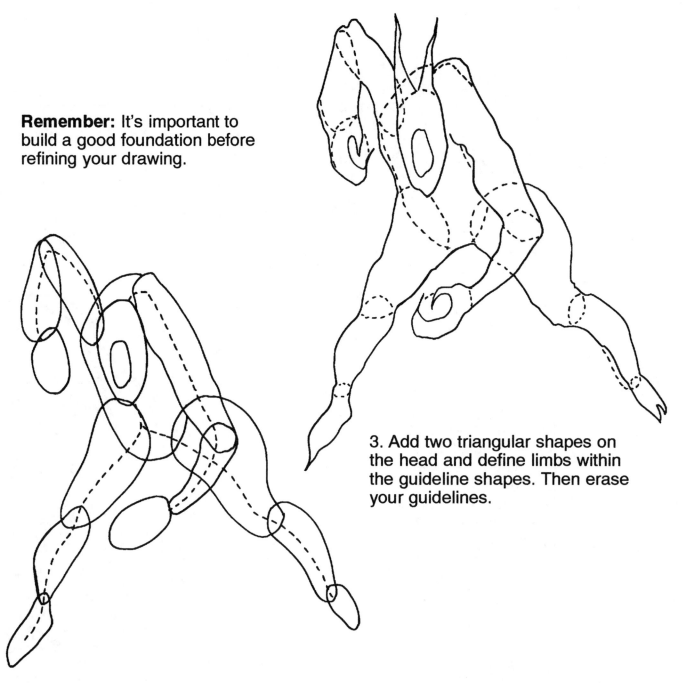

Remember: It's important to build a good foundation before refining your drawing.

3. Add two triangular shapes on the head and define limbs within the guideline shapes. Then erase your guidelines.

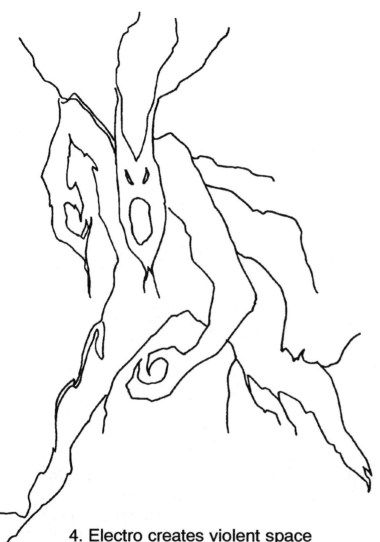

4. Electro creates violent space storms. Make the outline of Electro's limbs a continuous jagged line. Then attach lightning bolts from all parts of his body. Lightning is jagged and sharp, similar to many types of tree branches.

5. Add lots of lightning, and add a double or triple outline all around Electro's body. For a completely different effect, use white chalk to draw Electro on black paper. Then see how really scary he can get.

QUARK,
THE ATOM MASTER

Remember: Keep all your guidelines lightly drawn. They will be easier to erase later on.

1. & 2.
Draw an oval for the head and the basic stick figure. Add the triangle for the torso, and oval guideline shapes for arms and hands.

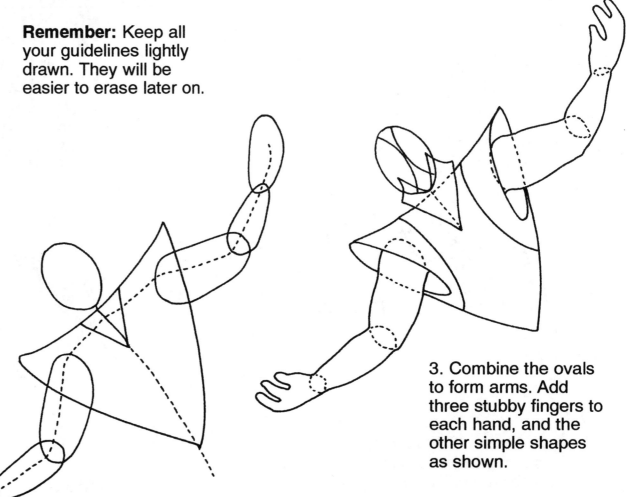

3. Combine the ovals to form arms. Add three stubby fingers to each hand, and the other simple shapes as shown.

4. Keep refining the arms and hands. Then complete the head and torso section. Blend all the lines and shapes, erasing unneeded guidelines as you go along. Then, add two long lines on each side of the head going towards the hands. At the end of each line, draw two intersecting ovals.

5. Add details and all the finishing touches to the Atom Master. Draw as many ovals around his waist as you wish. Keep drawing and erasing until you're satisfied with the way Quark looks.

SUB-GRUB

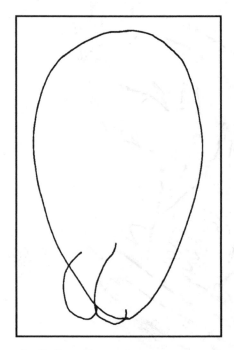

1. & 2.
Lightly sketch a giant oval and two curved fangs. Sub-Grub is definitely not smooth, so begin outlining its head with a jagged line.

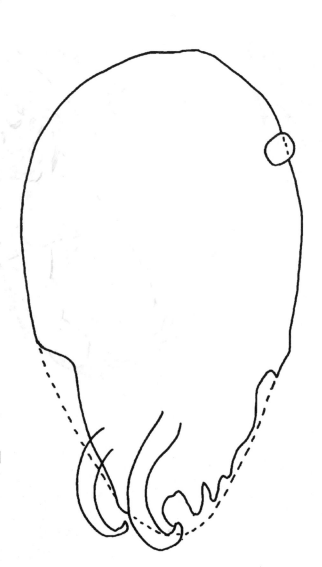

3. Create guidelines for the eyes and gaping mouth, and continue working on the head outline.

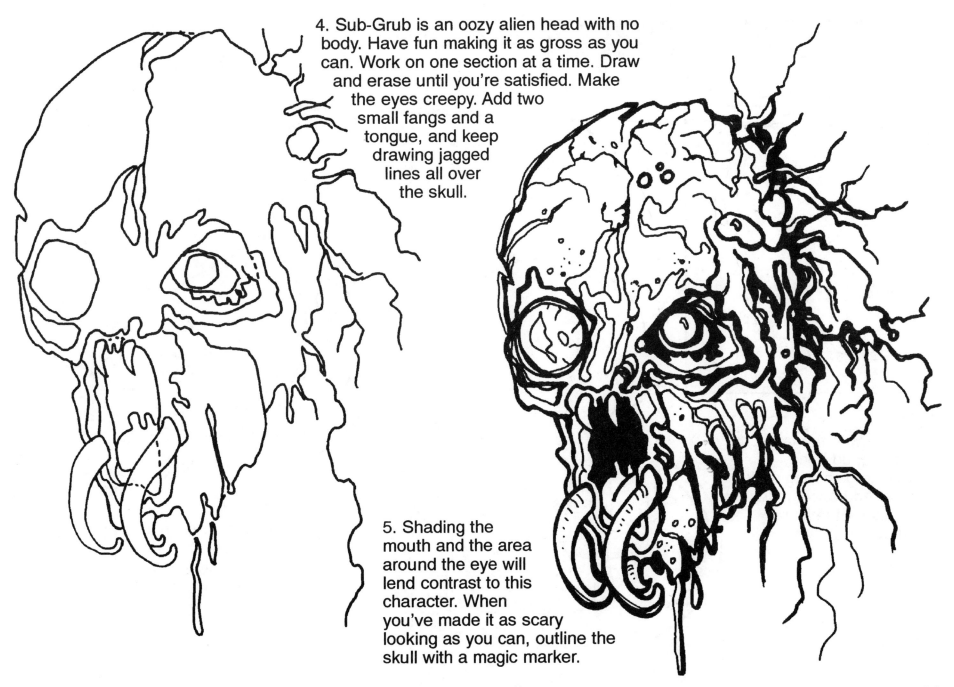

4. Sub-Grub is an oozy alien head with no body. Have fun making it as gross as you can. Work on one section at a time. Draw and erase until you're satisfied. Make the eyes creepy. Add two small fangs and a tongue, and keep drawing jagged lines all over the skull.

5. Shading the mouth and the area around the eye will lend contrast to this character. When you've made it as scary looking as you can, outline the skull with a magic marker.

ASTROID SPRITE

1. & 2.
Starting with the large, oval-shaped head, draw the gesturing stick figure. Add overlapping shapes for the limbs and tail.

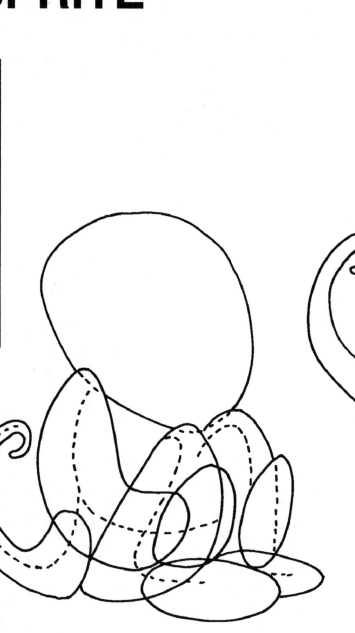

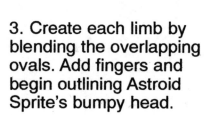

3. Create each limb by blending the overlapping ovals. Add fingers and begin outlining Astroid Sprite's bumpy head.

5. The Astroid Sprite is a shy creature who hides among asteroids and small moons. He's hard to spot because he resembles the texture of the surface he's sitting on. When you're finished with the final touches, use a thick marker to outline the entire drawing, or color him with some weird colors.

Remember: Be patient. Keep drawing and erasing until you're happy with your work.

4. Add facial features and draw different-sized bumps on the head. Then carefully blend the outline of the body. Erase any guidelines you no longer need.

STAR CRUISER

1. & 2. Start by drawing the guideline shapes for the craft's body and the four wings.

3. Add dividing lines on the front part of the Cruiser. Next, add the circular section beneath the front, and the tail section.

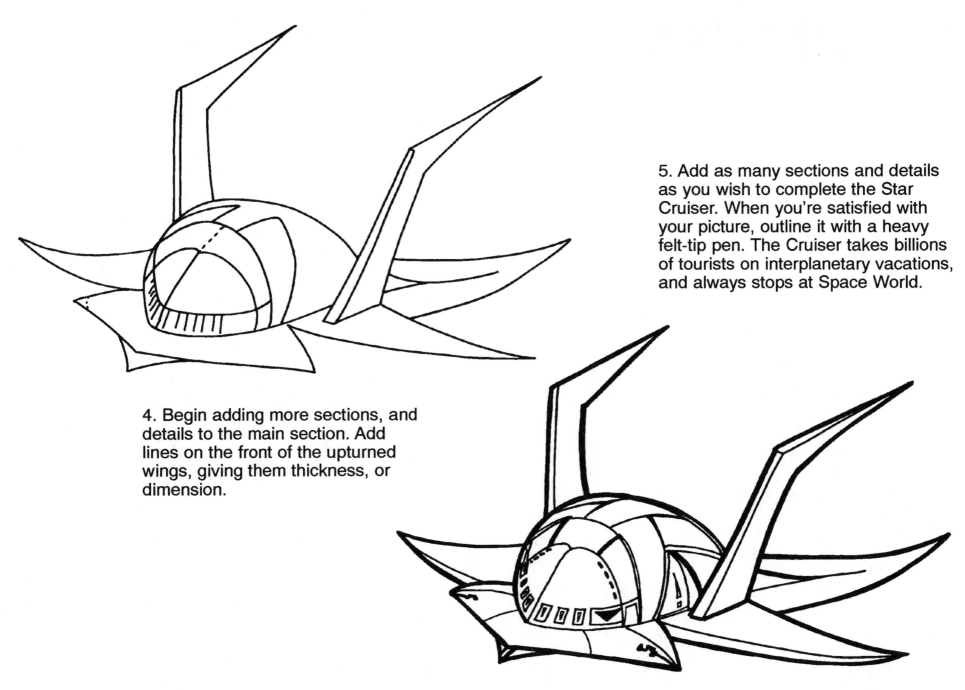

5. Add as many sections and details as you wish to complete the Star Cruiser. When you're satisfied with your picture, outline it with a heavy felt-tip pen. The Cruiser takes billions of tourists on interplanetary vacations, and always stops at Space World.

4. Begin adding more sections, and details to the main section. Add lines on the front of the upturned wings, giving them thickness, or dimension.

SPACE TITAN

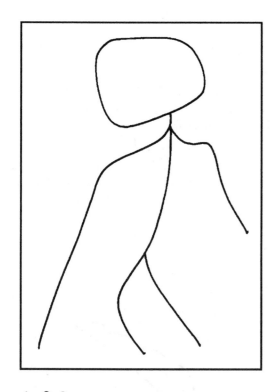

1. & 2.
Begin by lightly drawing the stick figure. Then add guideline shapes as shown. Draw the open mouth and four wavy lines coming from the head and shoulder.

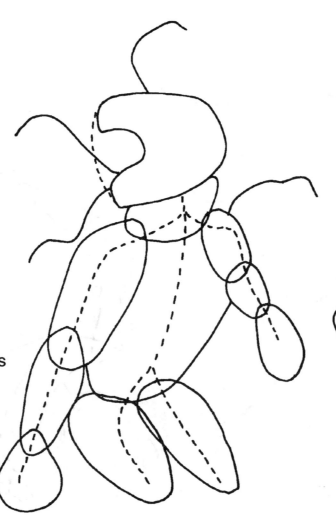

3. Define the heads and limbs within the guidelines and add horns to each head.

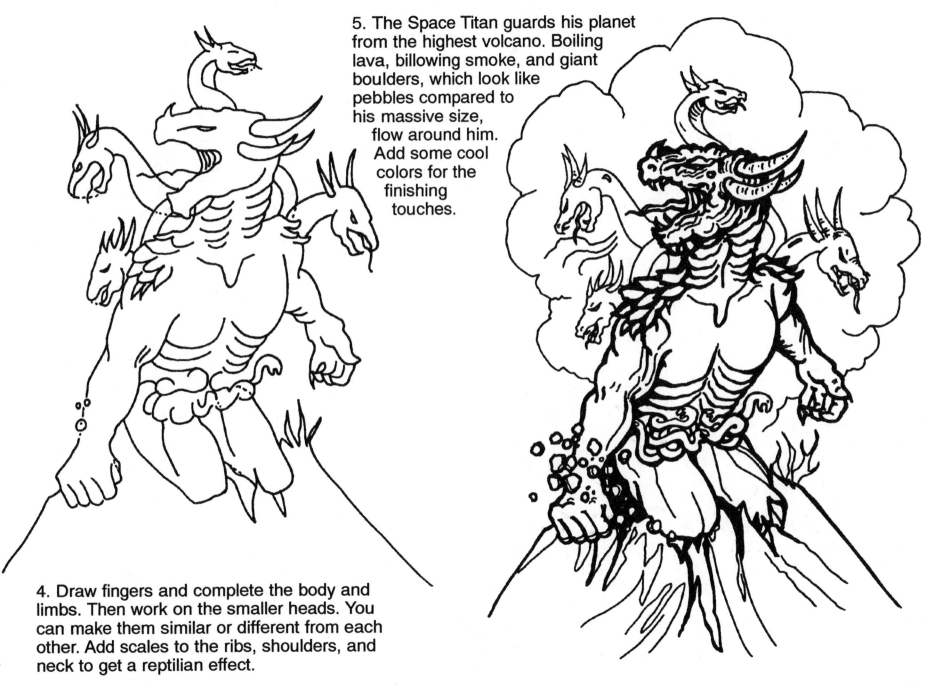

5. The Space Titan guards his planet from the highest volcano. Boiling lava, billowing smoke, and giant boulders, which look like pebbles compared to his massive size, flow around him. Add some cool colors for the finishing touches.

4. Draw fingers and complete the body and limbs. Then work on the smaller heads. You can make them similar or different from each other. Add scales to the ribs, shoulders, and neck to get a reptilian effect.

GORGO, THE WATCHER

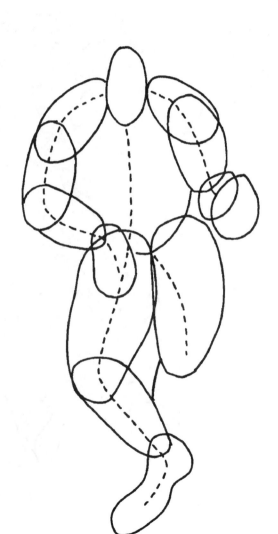

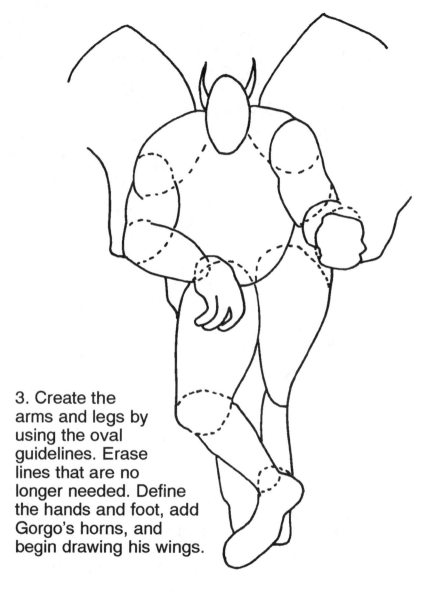

1. & 2.
Lightly sketch the gesturing stick figure. Then carefully add the overlapping ovals.

3. Create the arms and legs by using the oval guidelines. Erase lines that are no longer needed. Define the hands and foot, add Gorgo's horns, and begin drawing his wings.

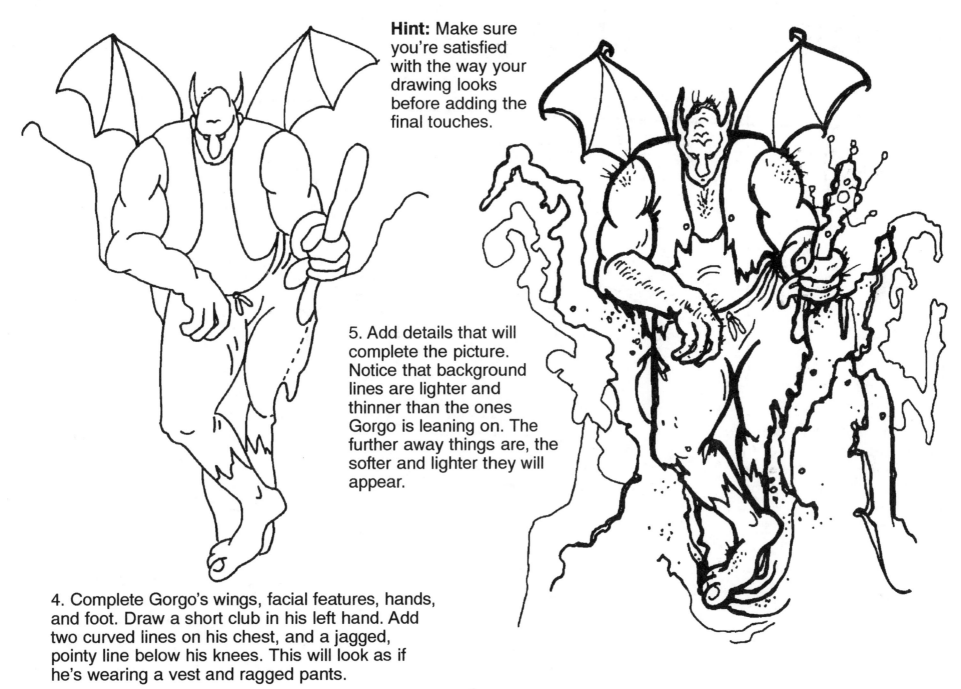

Hint: Make sure you're satisfied with the way your drawing looks before adding the final touches.

5. Add details that will complete the picture. Notice that background lines are lighter and thinner than the ones Gorgo is leaning on. The further away things are, the softer and lighter they will appear.

4. Complete Gorgo's wings, facial features, hands, and foot. Draw a short club in his left hand. Add two curved lines on his chest, and a jagged, pointy line below his knees. This will look as if he's wearing a vest and ragged pants.

SPACE MECHANIC

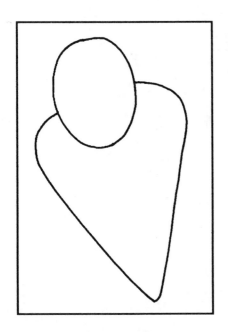

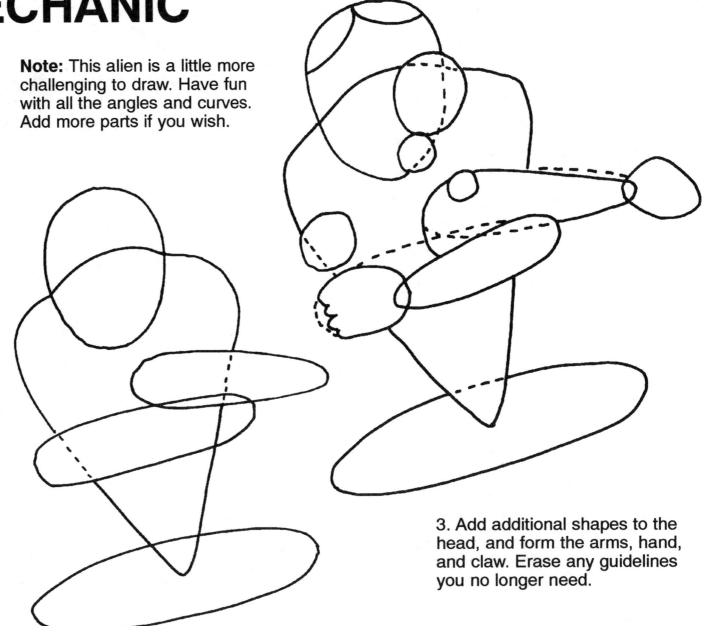

Note: This alien is a little more challenging to draw. Have fun with all the angles and curves. Add more parts if you wish.

1. & 2.
Draw the oval and V-shaped guidelines for the head and body. Then add three more ovals for the arms and the base.

3. Add additional shapes to the head, and form the arms, hand, and claw. Erase any guidelines you no longer need.

50

Remember: Always feel free to use your imagination when adding the final touches.

4. Work on one section at a time, starting with the head. Carefully draw the shapes on the face. Then add the curved bar going from shoulder to shoulder. Sketch the arm with the hand holding the phaser, then the one with the claw. Draw the lower body sections.

5. Add lots of details and shading to complete this picture. When all the finishing touches have been added, your Space Mechanic will be ready to make repairs.

SPACE WORLD

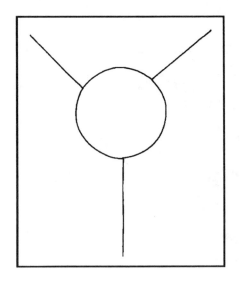

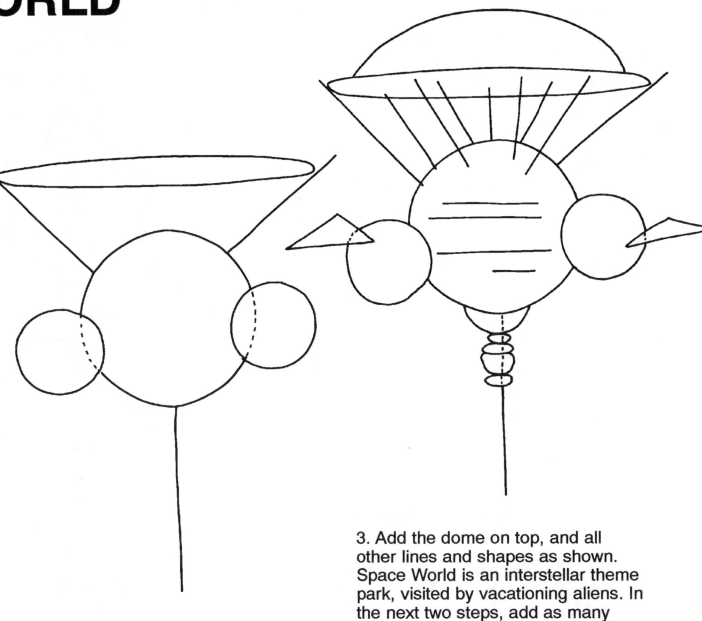

1. & 2.
Start with a circle and three straight lines. Then add the flat oval on top and a smaller circle on each side of the main circle.

Remember: Always draw your guidelines lightly in steps 1 and 2. It will be easier to erase them later.

3. Add the dome on top, and all other lines and shapes as shown. Space World is an interstellar theme park, visited by vacationing aliens. In the next two steps, add as many sections to the park as you like.

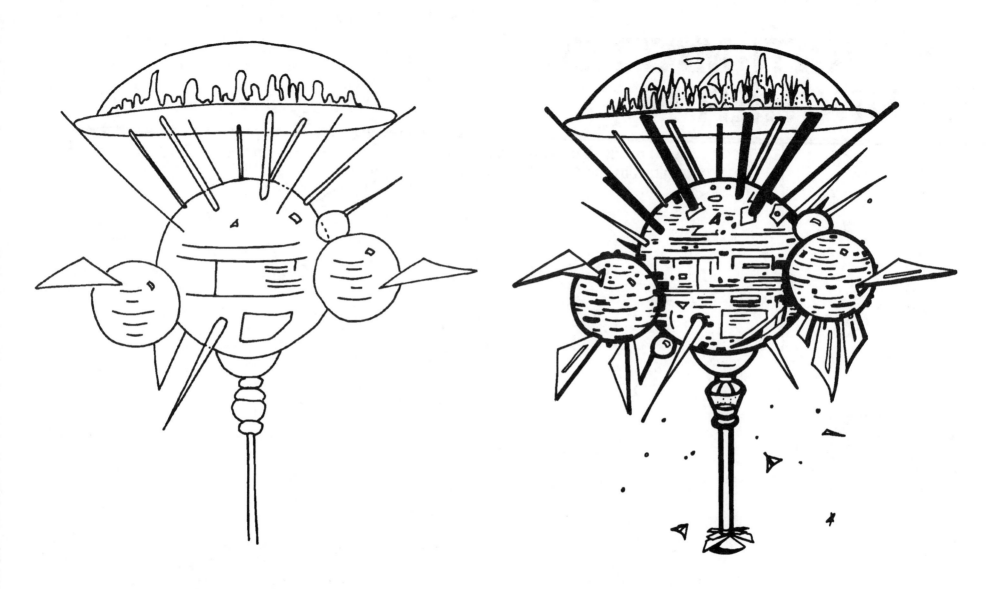

4. Add a skyline within the dome and keep drawing differently shaped sections on the circular parts.

5. When all the details and shading have been completed, use a magic marker for contrast and to highlight some sections.

THE ANTI-MATTER CRUNCHER

Remember: It's usually easier to begin with the largest shape first.

1. & 2.
Starting with the head, create the gesturing stick figure as shown. Then carefully add over-lapping oval body shapes.

3. Draw basic body shapes within the ovals. Now you have created a solid foundation which will make your drawing easier to complete. In the next two steps you are simply refining and adding shapes and details to the foundation.

4. Erase unnecessary guidelines as you blend the shapes. Starting with the head, add defining features of each section of the body.

5. Finish the Anti-Matter Cruncher by adding lots of details to its cosmic suit. Also, supply it with some matter to crunch. When you're done, outline your drawing with a heavy felt-tip pen and add some background.

SQUITCH

3. Form the legs and feet, and outline the head. Then sketch the five long, waving tentacles. On the head, add a few short tentacles, with circles on top. Keep erasing unneeded guidelines as you go along.

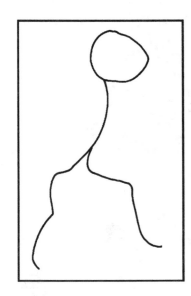

1. & 2.
Start by drawing the basic stick figure. Add oval guideline shapes for the body, the legs, and the feet. Then draw five wavy lines attached to the top of the body.

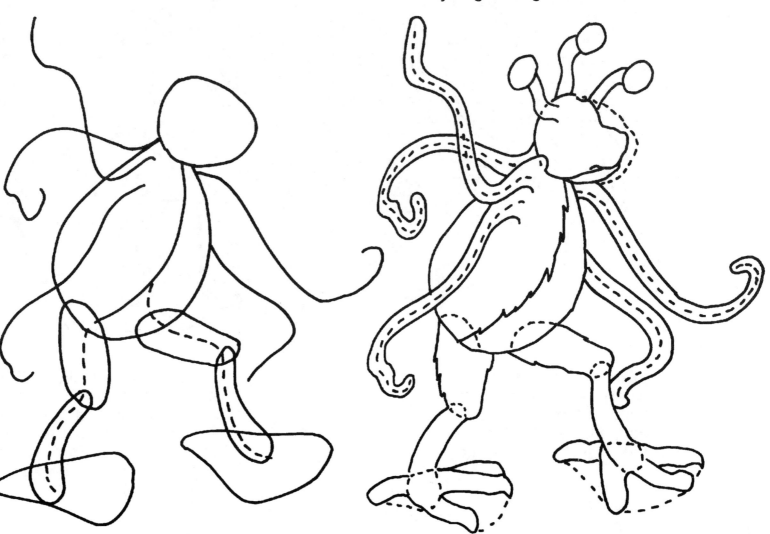

56

Hint: Don't be afraid to erase. It usually takes lots of drawing and erasing before you will be satisfied with the way this alien looks.

4. Refine the body, legs, and feet. Add two jagged, curved lines to the torso, and one on each leg. This will make the creature look fuzzy. Drawing a series of curved lines below the knee will look like scales.

5. Add short, curved lines near the eyes to make them appear to be in motion. Then add tiny ovals within ovals on the tentacles, and all the finishing touches that will complete your alien.

GLUGGO

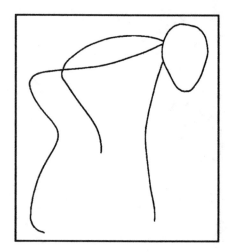

1. & 2.
Draw the basic line figure and all the overlapping oval shapes. Carve out an indentation for the mouth.

Remember: Take your time doing steps 1 and 2. If you get the basic foundation right, the rest of your drawing will be easy to do.

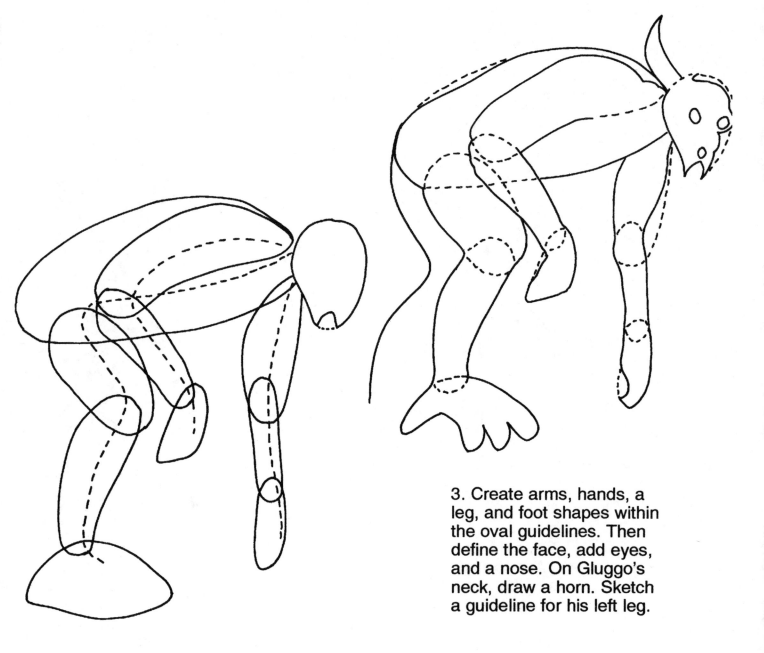

3. Create arms, hands, a leg, and foot shapes within the oval guidelines. Then define the face, add eyes, and a nose. On Gluggo's neck, draw a horn. Sketch a guideline for his left leg.

4. Blend the outline of the body so that it flows smoothly. Make the horn jagged and add a fin on the back. Work on hands, eyes, and mouth, and begin adding details.

5. The outline of Gluggo's body should be jagged and roughly drawn. Gluggo can be found in developing seas, covered with slimy seaweed. Make the water foamy and frothy, with lots of swirls and white caps.

MAGNETO

1. & 2.
Create the stick figure and all the free-form shapes attached to it.

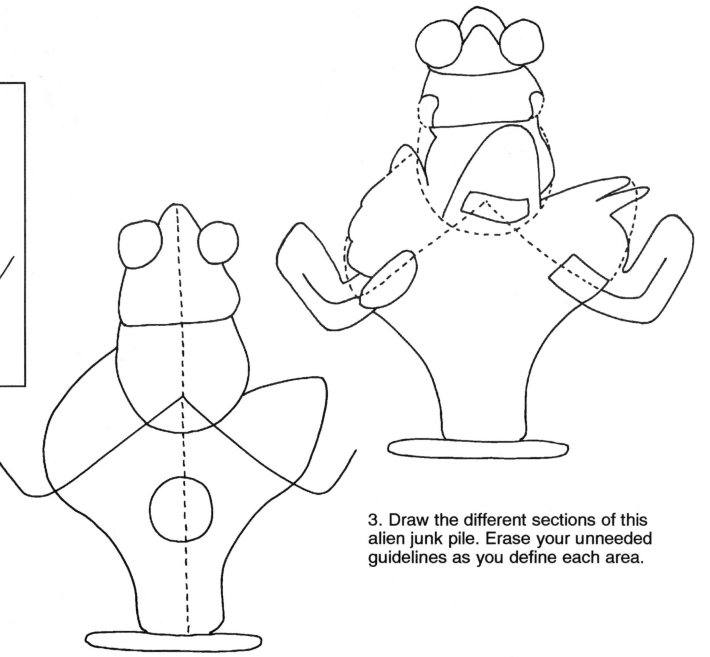

3. Draw the different sections of this alien junk pile. Erase your unneeded guidelines as you define each area.

4. Start adding debris to the body. Drawing several circles in the eyes will make them appear to be bulging out.

5. Magneto is a portable junk heap. Space debris and old rocket parts stick to this alien because it's super magnetic. Add as much debris as you like, in any shape or size. What you see here is only a guide.

UFO RESCUE SQUAD

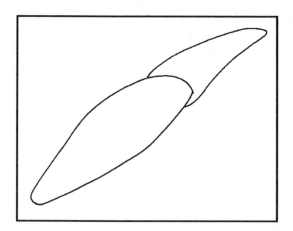

1. Lightly draw the two interlocking free-form shapes.

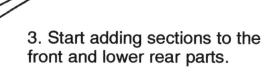

3. Start adding sections to the front and lower rear parts.

2. Sketch the two small ovals and the lower rear section. Then shape the front of the craft.

Remember: Use your imagination whenever drawing an imaginary object or creature.

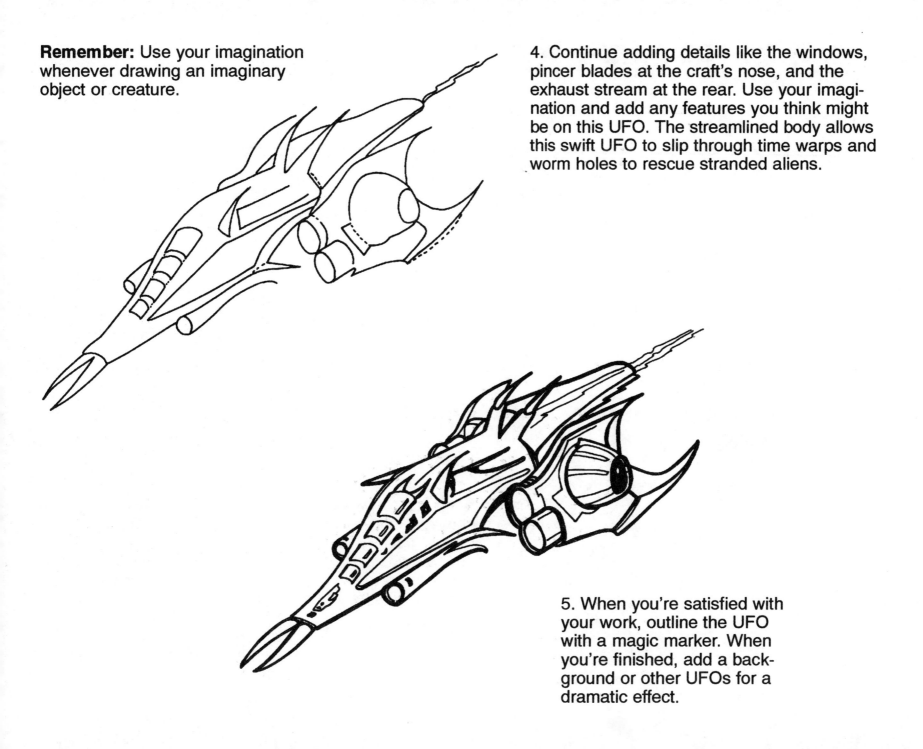

4. Continue adding details like the windows, pincer blades at the craft's nose, and the exhaust stream at the rear. Use your imagination and add any features you think might be on this UFO. The streamlined body allows this swift UFO to slip through time warps and worm holes to rescue stranded aliens.

5. When you're satisfied with your work, outline the UFO with a magic marker. When you're finished, add a background or other UFOs for a dramatic effect.

MANOS THE MENACE

1. & 2.
Starting with the oval-shaped head, draw the gesturing stick figure. Add overlapping shapes for the body and limbs.

Remember: Keep these guidelines lightly drawn.

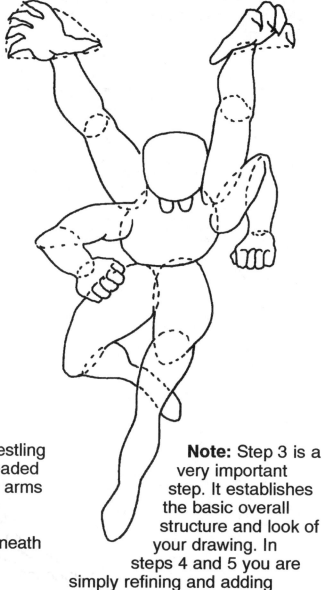

3. Manos is famous for wrestling space serpents and four-headed hydras. Define the muscular arms and legs within the guideline shapes. Draw fingers on four hands. Add two semi-circles beneath the head.

Note: Step 3 is a very important step. It establishes the basic overall structure and look of your drawing. In steps 4 and 5 you are simply refining and adding details to the figure you have created in step 3.

4. Connect and blend all the shapes into a smooth outline of the alien's body. Erase any unnecessary guidelines as you go along. Add details to the foot, the waist, the head, and one line down the center of the chest.

5. Add details, shading, and all the finishing touches and refinements. Don't forget the claws on Manos's feet and a cool pattern on his head.

COSMIC COBRA

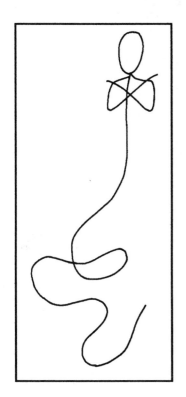

1. & 2.
Lightly sketch the basic stick figure by carefully drawing a long, curved line as shown. Add the snakelike guideline for the body.

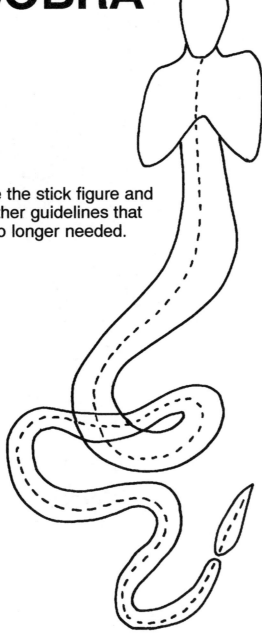

Erase the stick figure and the other guidelines that are no longer needed.

3. Define arm sections within the oval shapes and create the hood around the head. Add jagged shapes to both sides of the upper body.

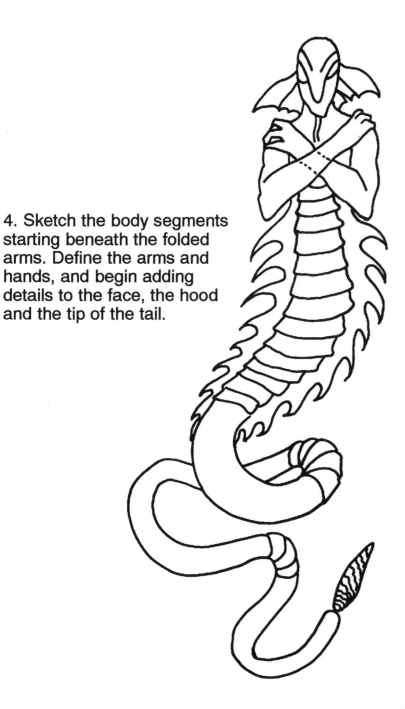

4. Sketch the body segments starting beneath the folded arms. Define the arms and hands, and begin adding details to the face, the hood and the tip of the tail.

5. Continue drawing the body segments. Note how they get rounder as they get smaller. Complete the face, and add horns, curved teeth, and a forked tongue. The Cosmic Cobra is now ready to snatch its favorite prey—a passing UFO!

SKORPIO SHUTTLE

1. Lightly sketch the large free-form shape and the four flowing lines.

Note: If at this point you're not satisfied with any part of your drawing, erase it and start over.

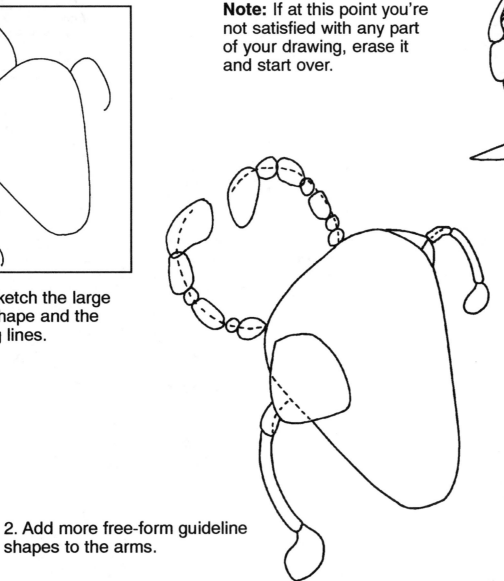

2. Add more free-form guideline shapes to the arms.

3. Create claws and define arm sections. This UFO is used for carrying supplies to space stations. The claws help it to lift and load materials. Draw the two flaps at the top end of the body and the cut-out shapes on the front.

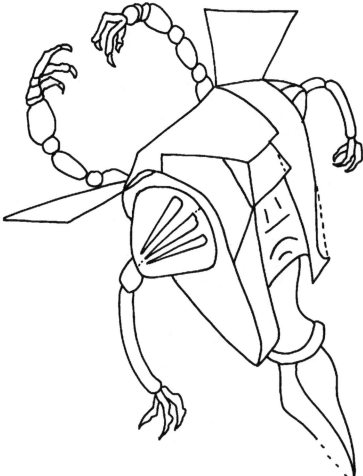

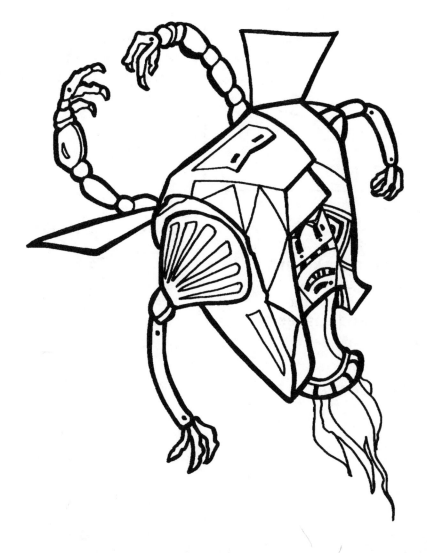

5. Add all the details and finishing touches that will complete your drawing. Have fun adding extra eyes, shapes, and patterns if you wish. Now the Skorpio Shuttle is ready to zoom away on another mission.

4. Add more sections to the main body—use your imagination and draw as many as you wish. Add a "face" in the middle of the body and some exhaust lines at the bottom. Continue to refine the arms and claws.

COMETO

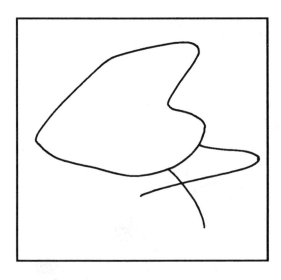

1. & 2.
Begin by lightly sketching a free-form guideline shape. Then draw the other lines and shapes as shown.

Remember: The dotted lines are guidelines you no longer need and can be erased.

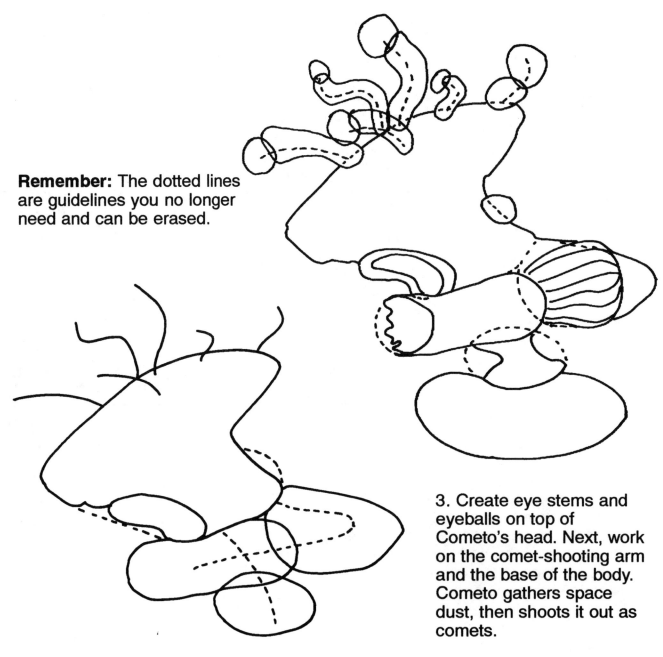

3. Create eye stems and eyeballs on top of Cometo's head. Next, work on the comet-shooting arm and the base of the body. Cometo gathers space dust, then shoots it out as comets.

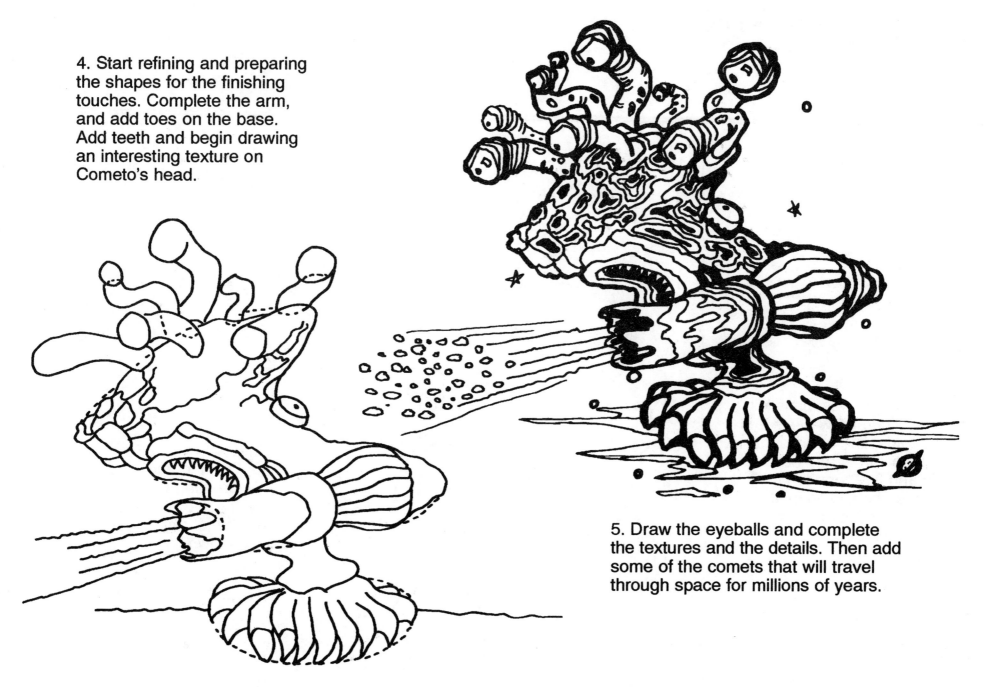

4. Start refining and preparing the shapes for the finishing touches. Complete the arm, and add toes on the base. Add teeth and begin drawing an interesting texture on Cometo's head.

5. Draw the eyeballs and complete the textures and the details. Then add some of the comets that will travel through space for millions of years.

71

LUNATICKY

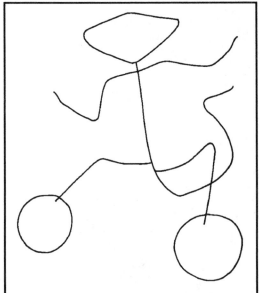

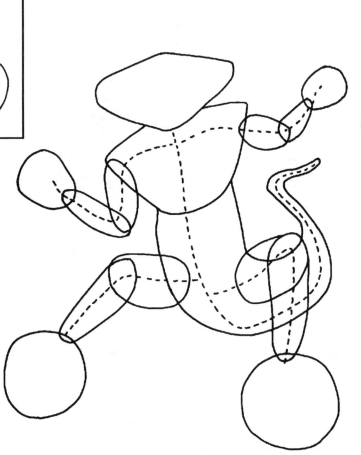

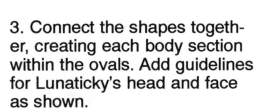

1. & 2.
Begin with the simple stick figure. Then draw ovals and other guideline shapes for the body, arms and hands, legs and feet, and long tail. By carefully adding oval shapes over the stick figure, you have created a solid foundation.

3. Connect the shapes together, creating each body section within the ovals. Add guidelines for Lunaticky's head and face as shown.

4. Add the nose, eyes, and wavy tongue, and a series of curved spikes on the head. Next, create the sections on the snakelike body. Then carefully draw the clawed hands and feet. Add a few circles in the background.

5. For the finishing touches, add as many details to this alien as you like. When you're finished, use a thick marker to outline the entire drawing. Or color Lunaticky with the weirdest colors you have.

Note: This alien may appear difficult to draw, but if you follow along carefully, step-by-step, you will be able to draw almost anything. It takes patience, practice, and lots of erasing to get it just right.

ACCORDIANO

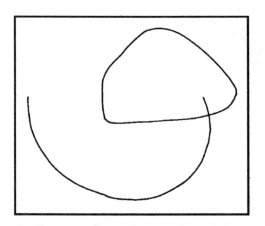

1. Draw a free-form triangular shape for the head and a large semi-circle for the tail.

3. Starting at the head and going down two-thirds of the way, draw a bumpy line on both sides of the tail. Add a guideline shape for the eyebrow.

2. Carve out the head and mouth. Using the guidelines, sketch a tail with a pointy tip.

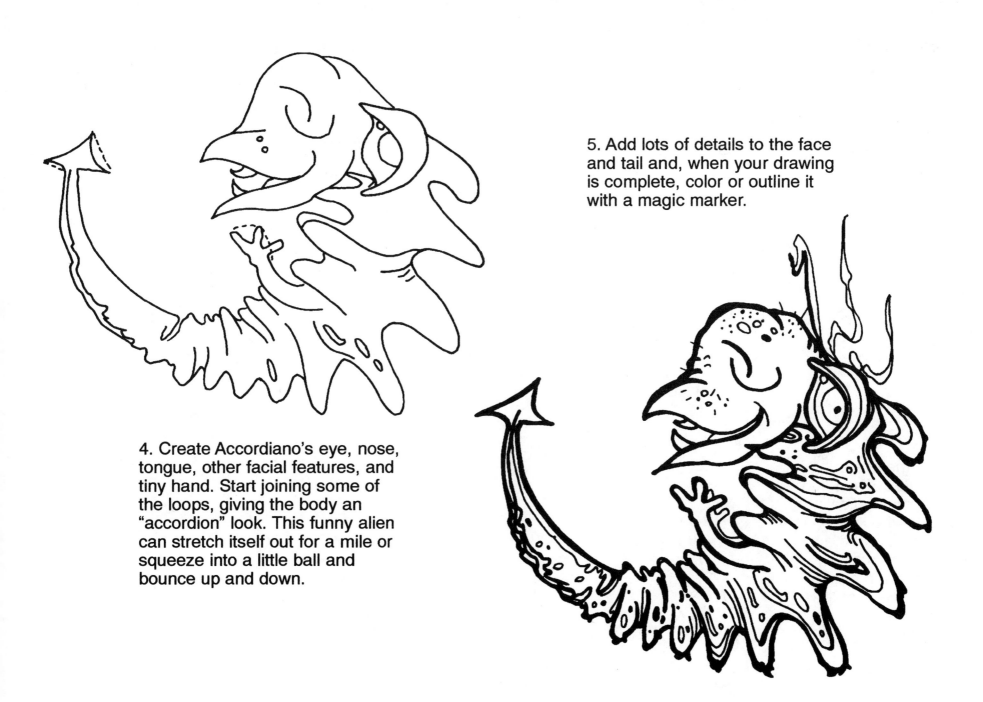

5. Add lots of details to the face and tail and, when your drawing is complete, color or outline it with a magic marker.

4. Create Accordiano's eye, nose, tongue, other facial features, and tiny hand. Start joining some of the loops, giving the body an "accordion" look. This funny alien can stretch itself out for a mile or squeeze into a little ball and bounce up and down.

CRAZO

1. & 2.
Create the gesturing stick figure. Then add overlapping guideline ovals for the limbs. Add claws and draw two circles for the eyes. Start to carve out the shape of the head.

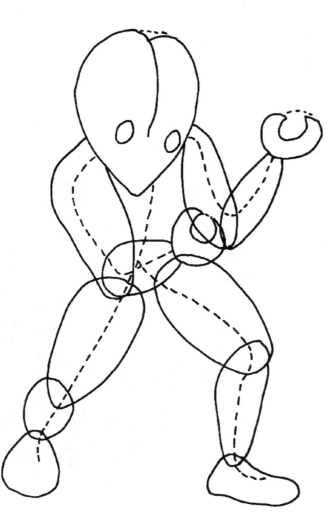

3. Define the muscular arms and legs within the ovals. Keep working until you have a smooth outline of Crazo's body. Add clawed toes on the right foot and another ring of circles around the eyes. Erase any guidelines you no longer need.

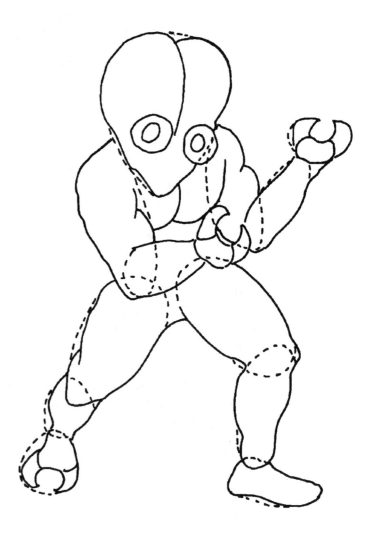

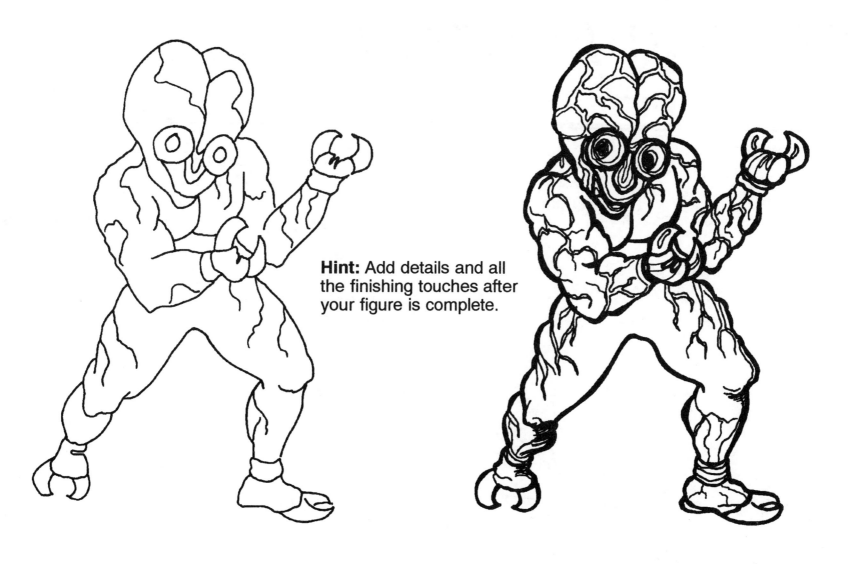

Hint: Add details and all the finishing touches after your figure is complete.

4. Add clawed toes on the left foot and begin drawing slightly jagged, small lines on the body for skin texture. Crazo doesn't have real skin—just a covering of membranes and goo.

5. Complete the eyes, nose, and skin. When you're satisfied with the way Crazo looks, color this alien with some fantastic colors.

SQUID FIGHTER CRAFT

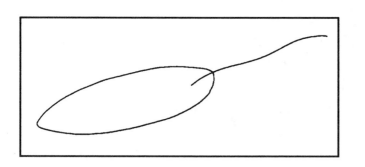

1. Start with a huge oval and a long, slightly wavy line.

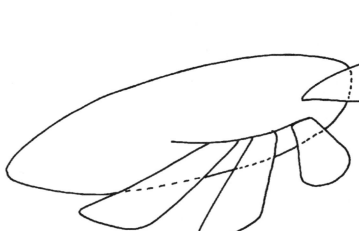

2. Draw three large oars on the lower section, and the flowing arm on the front.

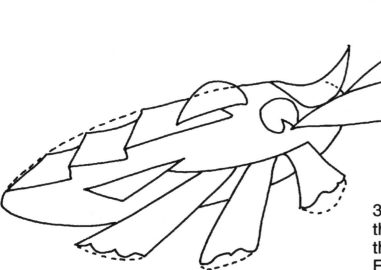

3. Create three steps on the upper left side of the craft and add another flowing shape at the front end. Define the edges of the oars. Erase any unneeded guidelines. On the body of the craft, add other details as shown.

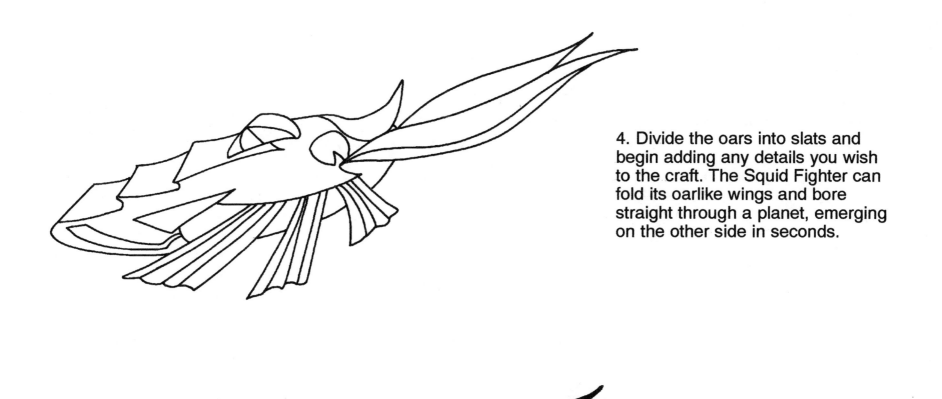

4. Divide the oars into slats and begin adding any details you wish to the craft. The Squid Fighter can fold its oarlike wings and bore straight through a planet, emerging on the other side in seconds.

5. Add all the final details and the finishing touches. When you are satisfied with the way your UFO looks, outline it with a felt-tip pen.

TORMENTO

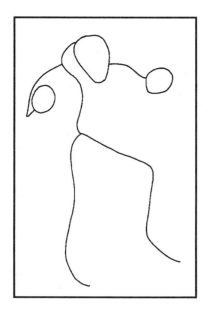

Note: Take your time doing steps 1 and 2. If you get the basic foundation right, the rest of your drawing will be easy to do.

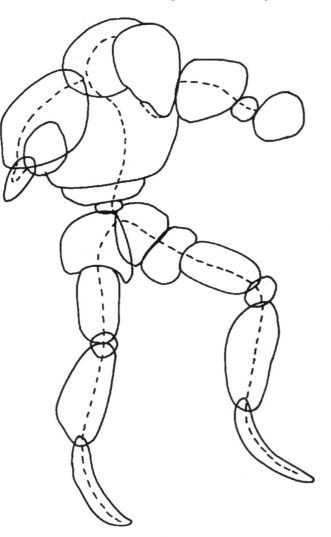

1. & 2.
Lightly sketch the basic line figure. Then, starting with the torso, carefully add overlapping guideline shapes for the upper body. Next, add ovals for the lower part. Start to carve out the shape of the head.

3. Combine the shapes, erasing unneeded guidelines as you go along. Begin defining the sections on the face, neck, arms, and waist.

4. Add antennae, fangs, and claws, and start sketching the finishing touches. Tormento has a poisonous bite, and is part robot, part nasty insect.

5. Complete Tormento by adding details, a dark outline, and your favorite colors.

SKORKKA

1. & 2.
Draw the gesturing stick figure and the overlapping guideline ovals. Make sure the figure is turned in the direction you wish. Start to carve out the shape of the head.

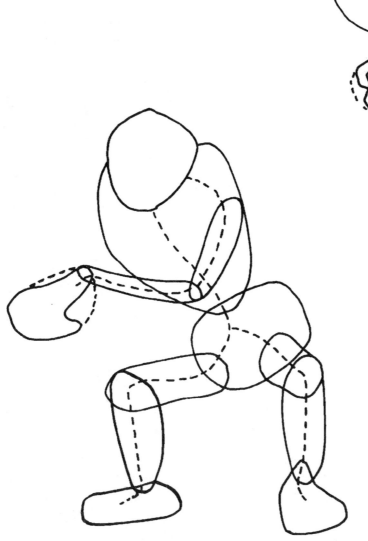

3. Create the legs, left arm, and left hand within the ovals. Add guidelines for the facial features, right arm, and right hand.

Note: Keep drawing and erasing until you are satisfied with the way Skorkka looks.

4. Sketch the right arm and hand. Then work on Skorkka's curved trunk, tusks, and other parts of the head.

5. Add details that will complete your picture. Remember, what you see here is only a guide. Always feel free to use your imagination when adding the finishing touches.

ZIGGITY ZOG, SPACE GUIDE

3. Start defining and shaping the arms, legs, hands, and feet within the oval guide lines. Erase the gesture lines as you go along. Then, add the guidelines for the facial features.

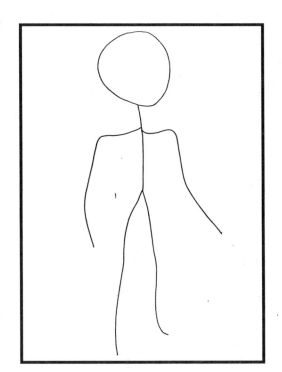

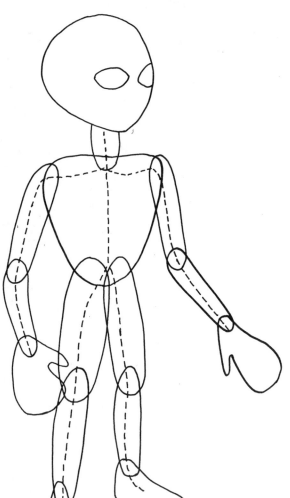

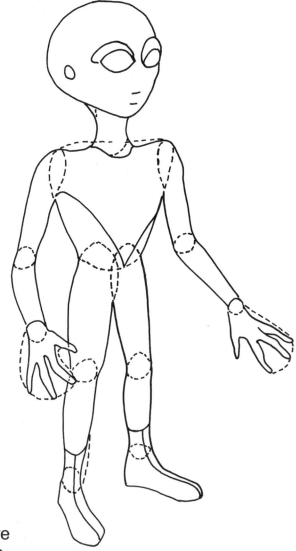

1.& 2. Starting with the head, draw the simple stick figure (gesture lines). Then add the various ovals and other guideline shapes.

Hint: Draw these key steps carefully. Get the stick figure to gesture in the directions you want it to. By carefully adding the ovals over the stick figure, you have created a solid foundation. This will give your figure a more realistic look after you've completed the next steps.

4. Complete the facial features. Then, blend and refine all the shapes into a smooth body outline of the alien and its body suit. Note the droopy skin lines on Ziggity Zog's neck.

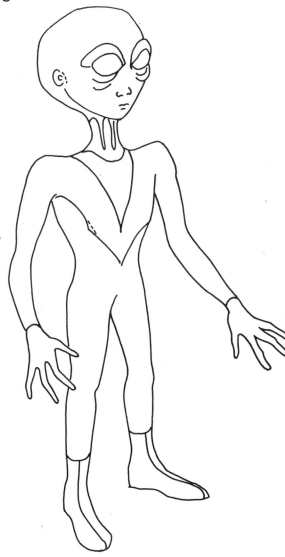

5. For the finishing touches, add details to the body suit, face, and fingertips. When your drawing is complete, use a heavy felt-tip pen to outline the figure, or color it with your favorite colors.

Before going to the next step, make sure that you are satisfied with the way your drawing looks.

MUDDY BUG SLUG

Erase any unnecessary guidelines as you go along.

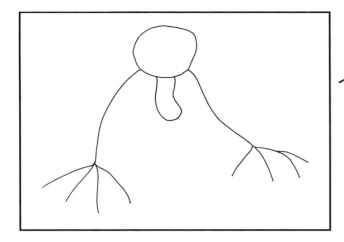

1. & 2.
Begin by lightly drawing the basic line figure. Then, add the ovals and other guideline shapes, as shown.

Always keep your pencil lines light and soft, so that the guidelines will be easier to erase when you no longer need them.

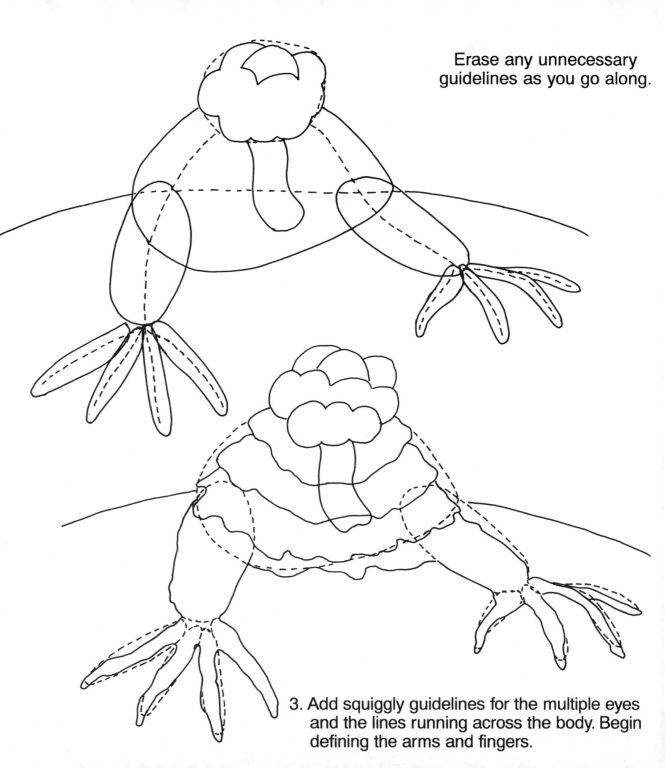

3. Add squiggly guidelines for the multiple eyes and the lines running across the body. Begin defining the arms and fingers.

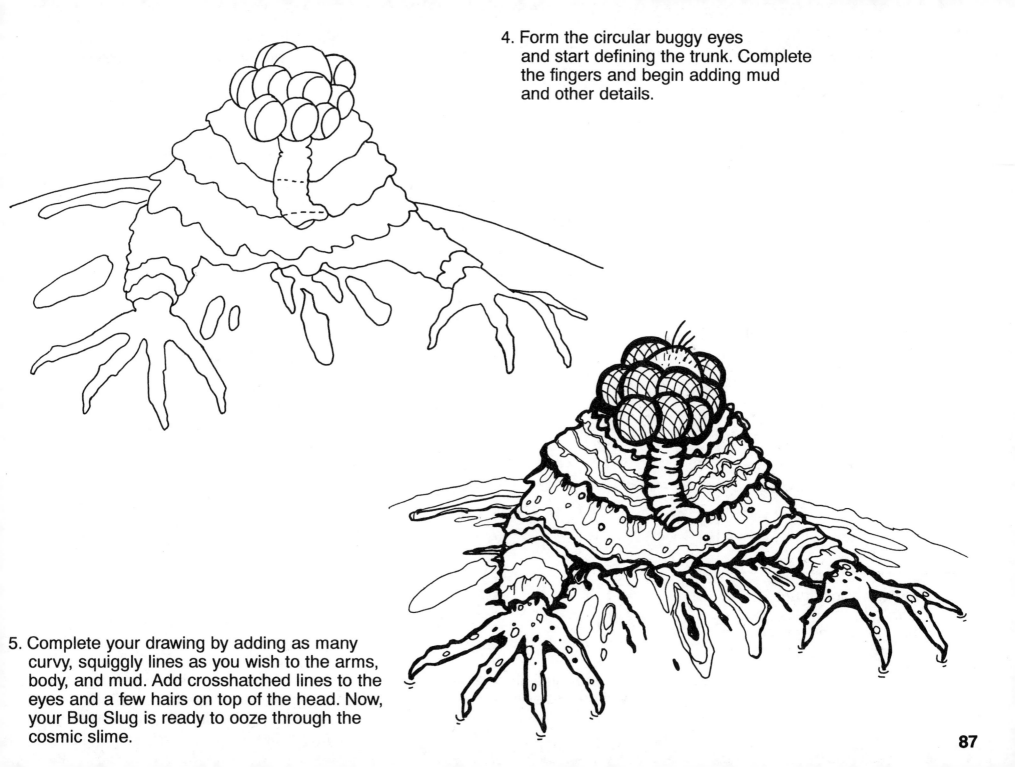

4. Form the circular buggy eyes and start defining the trunk. Complete the fingers and begin adding mud and other details.

5. Complete your drawing by adding as many curvy, squiggly lines as you wish to the arms, body, and mud. Add crosshatched lines to the eyes and a few hairs on top of the head. Now, your Bug Slug is ready to ooze through the cosmic slime.

NEPTOONIE, GALACTIC WATCHDOG

Note: If at this point you're not satisfied with any part of your drawing, erase and start again.

1. & 2. Draw the stick figure. Then, add the ovals and other guidelines for the disk, legs, and tentacles.

Hint: Keep all your guidelines lightly drawn. They will be easier to erase later on.

3. Add the additional shapes to the disk and complete the tentacle guidelines. Erase the stick figure and any guidelines you no longer need.

4. Add the curved lines and oval suction cups to the tentacles. Curving the lines will make the tentacles look round. Begin defining the "eye" stalk, and start adding details to your drawing.

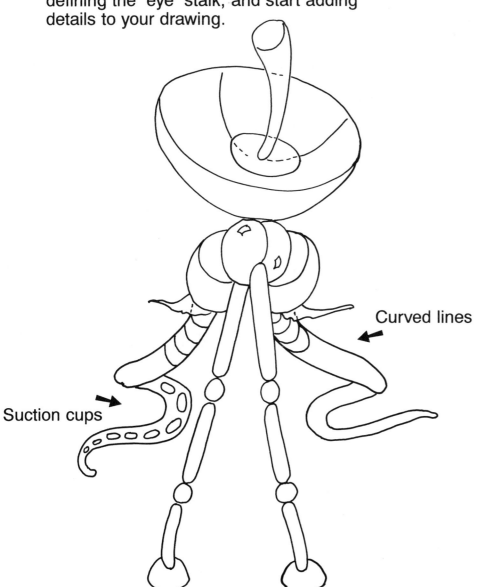

Curved lines

Suction cups

5. Complete the tentacles and add details to Neptoonie's legs, disk, and eye. When all the finishing touches have been added, your Galactic Watchdog will be ready for duty.

MADAME VENUSIAN

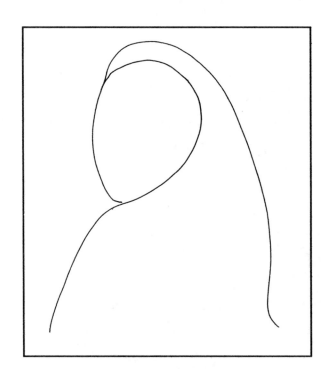

1. Begin with a lightly drawn oval shape for the face. Add the guide- lines for the shoulder and hair.

2. Add more guidelines for the hairline and facial features.

3. Begin defining the eyes, nose, and wavy hair. Keep erasing and drawing until the outlines are "just right."

Note: Make sure that the face is properly turned, looking over the shoulder. This is the most important part of building the foundation. It's easy to draw almost anything, if you first build a good foundation.

90

4. Carefully complete the facial features. Pay close attention to the connections between all the features—the eyebrow, pointy ear, and jaw line, for example. Define the ear, and continue adding the wavy hair.

5. Complete the hair, and start refining and adding all the face markings. Add any markings you wish. When you're satisfied with your drawing, color Madame Venusian with your wildest colors.

SPACE CITY OF VOORTEKKS

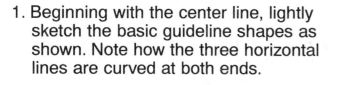

Center line

1. Beginning with the center line, lightly sketch the basic guideline shapes as shown. Note how the three horizontal lines are curved at both ends.

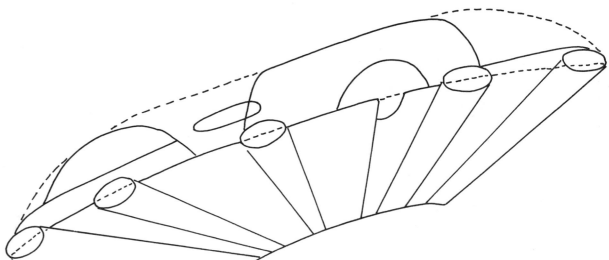

2. Add five small ovals on the center line. Then, draw lines from the ovals to the bottom of the ship. The lines should be closer to each other at the bottom. This will add depth and dimension to the Space City. Create the oval guideline shapes above the center line.

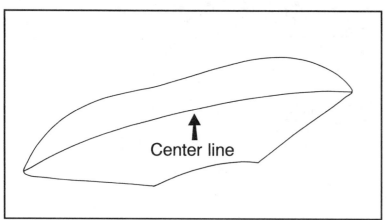

Round edges

Erase any unnecessary guidelines as you go along.

3. The top of this UFO is a city. Add additional shapes atop the center line to depict the domes, towers, and other structures. The ones shown here are just examples of how the city might look. Use your imagination, and add some structures of your own design.

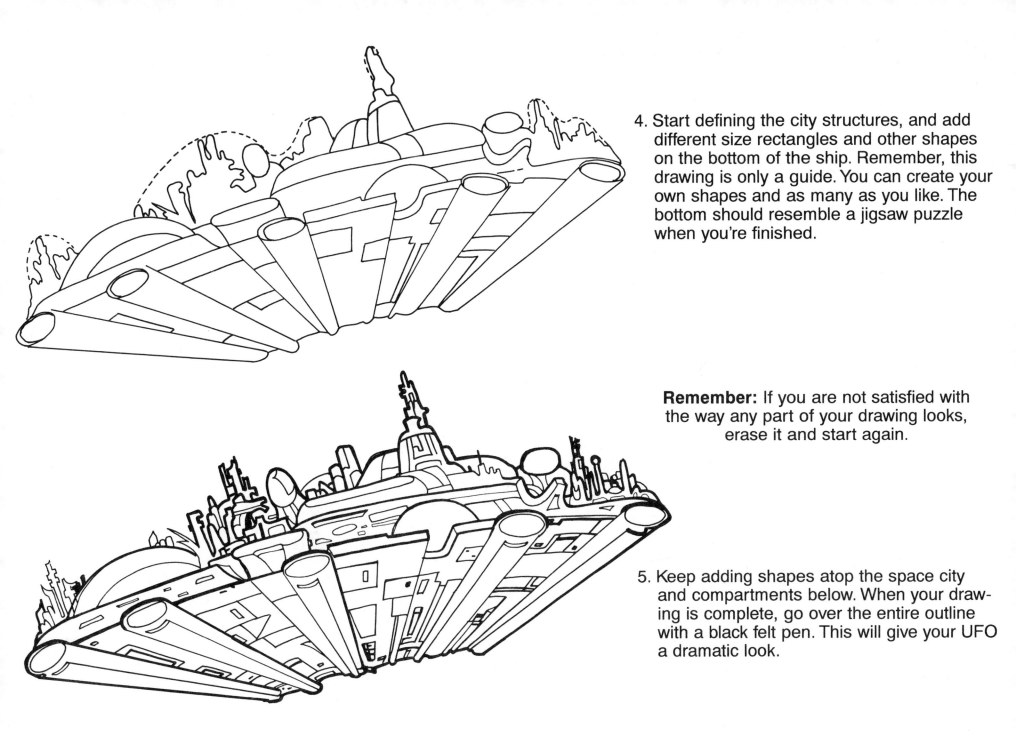

4. Start defining the city structures, and add different size rectangles and other shapes on the bottom of the ship. Remember, this drawing is only a guide. You can create your own shapes and as many as you like. The bottom should resemble a jigsaw puzzle when you're finished.

Remember: If you are not satisfied with the way any part of your drawing looks, erase it and start again.

5. Keep adding shapes atop the space city and compartments below. When your drawing is complete, go over the entire outline with a black felt pen. This will give your UFO a dramatic look.

MARTIAN GUARD

3. Create the body shapes within the ovals, and add additional guidelines for the flowing clothes. Begin forming the heads.

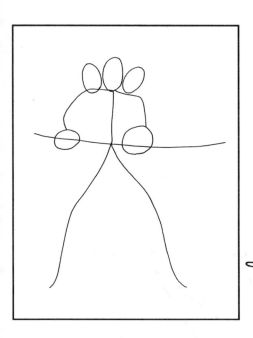

1. & 2. Draw the line figure and the oval guide-line shapes. Be extra careful as you overlap all the ovals. Add the guidelines for the sword.

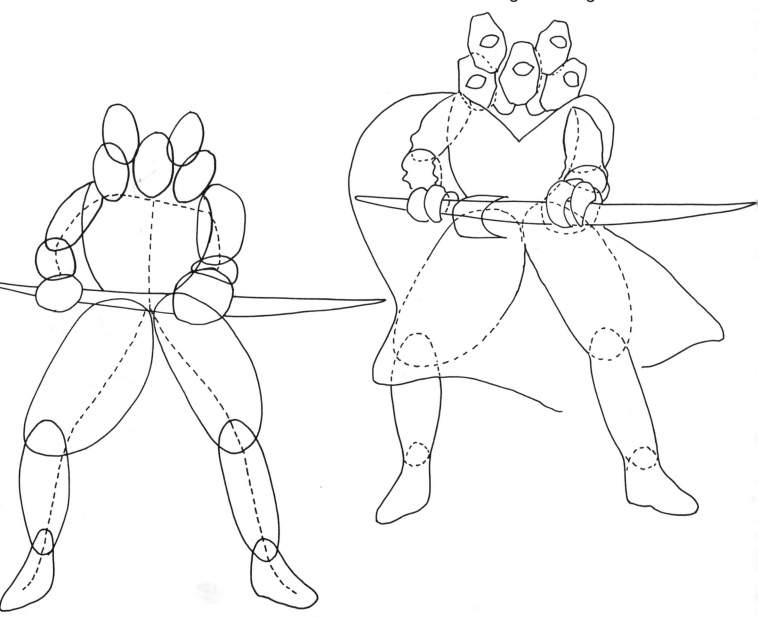

4. Blend the body parts together, erasing any guidelines you no longer need. Complete the clothes, and add details to the hands and boots. Add mouths and eyeballs to the five heads. The mouths should be different shapes and the eyes looking in all directions. Lastly, add flames around the heads.

5. Complete the faces, and add all the details and finishing touches. Now, with its sword at the ready, this Martian Guard is ready to take on intruders.

PHANTOM UFO

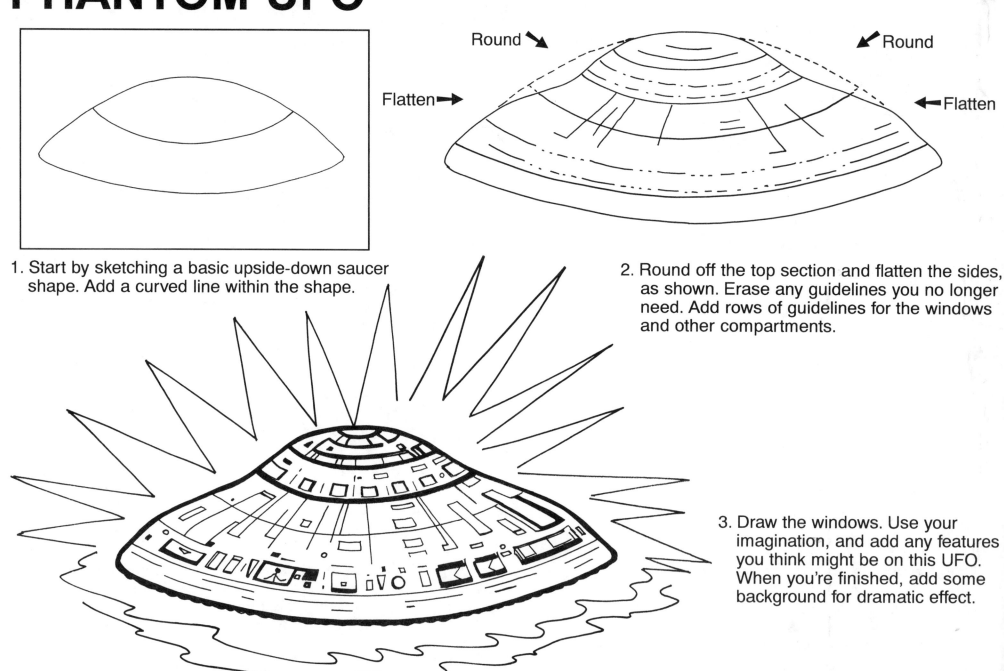

1. Start by sketching a basic upside-down saucer shape. Add a curved line within the shape.

Round

Flatten

Round

Flatten

2. Round off the top section and flatten the sides, as shown. Erase any guidelines you no longer need. Add rows of guidelines for the windows and other compartments.

3. Draw the windows. Use your imagination, and add any features you think might be on this UFO. When you're finished, add some background for dramatic effect.

Tear On Perforated Line

ALIEN STEALTH FIGHTER

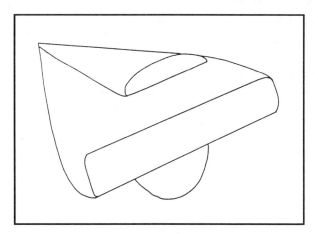

1. Draw the outline of the craft using basic guideline shapes.

2. Lightly sketch the guideline shapes for the different sections. Take it one section at a time, and as you complete each section, erase any unnecessary guidelines.

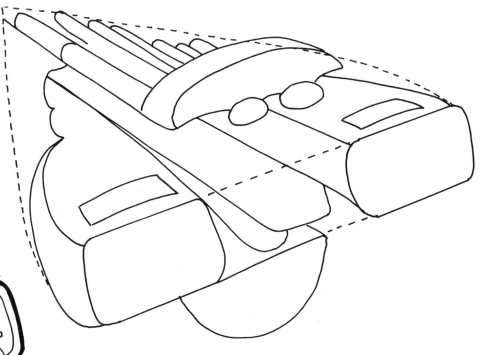

3. Blend the shapes together, refining and erasing as you go along. Keep adding lots of windows, hatches, and other details to the Alien Fighter until you are satisfied with the way it looks.

ALIEN ASTRONAUT

1. Starting with the oval-shaped head, draw the stick figure.

Remember: Keep these guidelines lightly drawn.

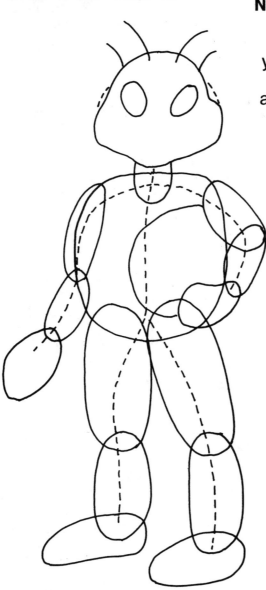

2. Add the overlapping body shapes, and the outlines of the helmet. Shape the face.

Note: Step 3 is a very important step. It establishes the basic overall structure and look of your drawing. In steps 4 and 5 you are simply refining and adding details to the figure you have created in step 3.

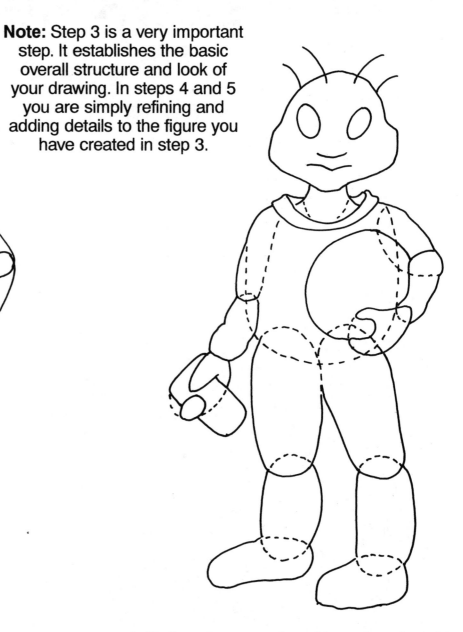

3. Define the arms, hands, and neck. Add guidelines for the nose and mouth, and the communicator in his right hand.

98

Always use your imagination when adding details. It's also fun to create a scene with several aliens in it.

4. Now you're ready for the final stages of your drawing. Connect and blend all the shapes together, erasing unnecessary guidelines as you go along. Draw the space suit and boots, facial features, and details to the helmet.

5. Add the details and all the finishing touches. Don't forget his antennas. You may want to color the Alien Astronaut when you're done.

ROBOWORM

Erase the stick figure and the other guidelines that are no longer needed.

1. & 2. After creating the basic stick figure, add the overlapping ovals and other body guideline shapes.

3. Define the arm sections within the oval shapes and create the claws. Shape the head, adding eye and mouth guidelines. Don't forget the robotic nose.

Starting at the top of the wormlike body behind the left arm, lightly sketch the body segments all the way down to the tip of the tail. Notice how the sections get rounder as they get smaller.

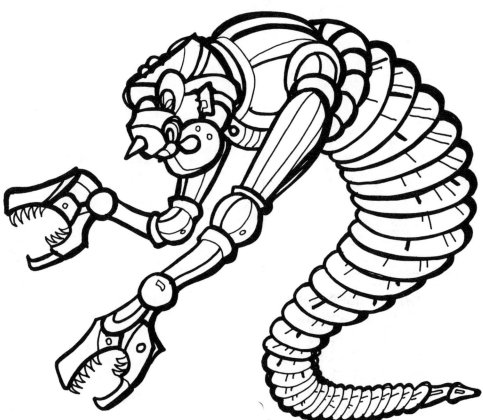

5. Add more details to the claws, face, and body. The short lines running down the body segments suggest a metallic look. Roboworm likes to burrow into asteroids to search for his favorite food—metal!

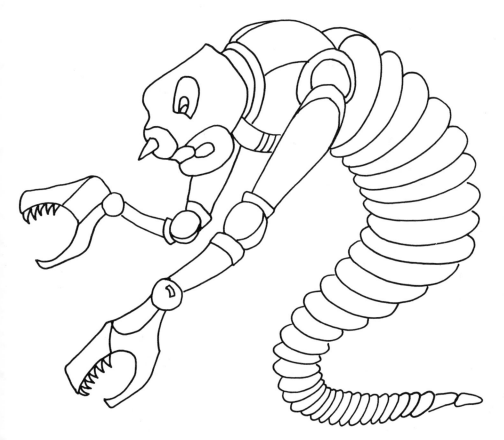

4. Complete the claws and elbows, and start adding details to the face and upper body. When you're satisfied with your drawing, begin adding the finishing touches.

HAIRY-ETTA

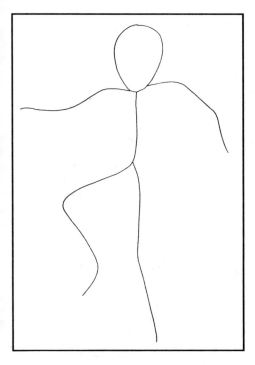

1. & 2. Draw the gesturing stick figure and the guideline shapes around it. It's usually easier to start at the top and work down, especially when so many of the ovals overlap.

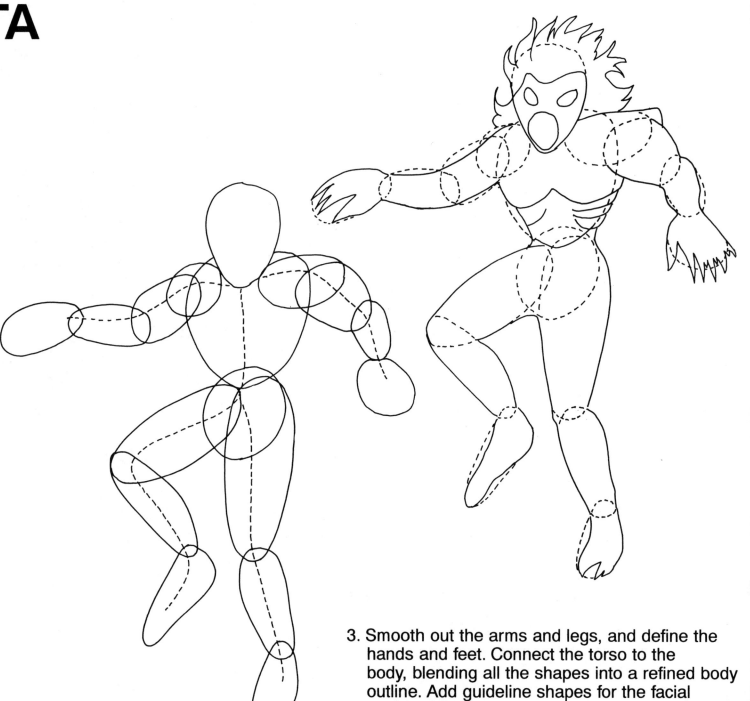

3. Smooth out the arms and legs, and define the hands and feet. Connect the torso to the body, blending all the shapes into a refined body outline. Add guideline shapes for the facial features and hair.

Hint: Add details and all the finishing touches **after** you have blended and refined the shapes.

4. Complete Hairy-etta's facial features, and begin adding details to her jacket. Then, draw the rows of jagged lines on her arms, hands, and body, as shown.

5. Add more jagged lines on her legs and feet. Finish the face, and continue adding details, until this creature from the Planet of the Fuzzies is complete.

COSMIC BOMB DETECTOR

1. & 2. Create the gesturing stick figure as shown. Then, carefully add the overlapping oval body shapes.

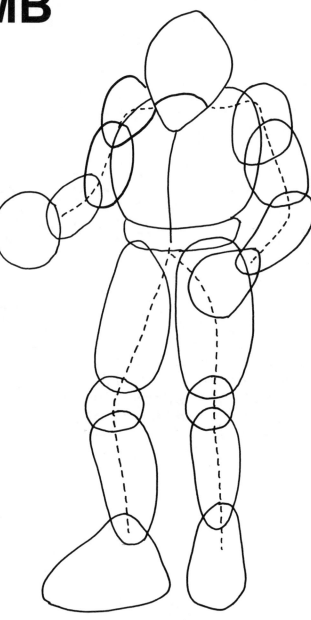

Remember to keep your guidelines lightly drawn.

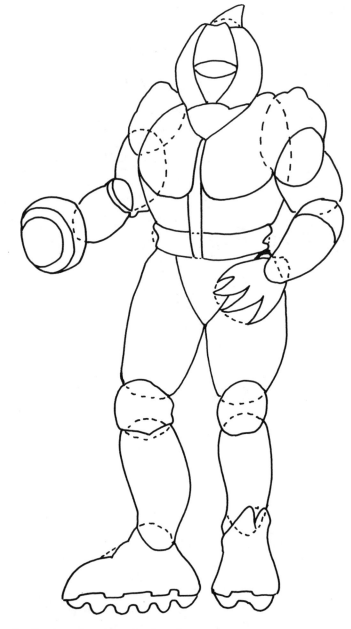

3. Draw the basic body shapes within the ovals, and start outlining the head, hands, and feet. Use a series of circles for the detector in the right hand.

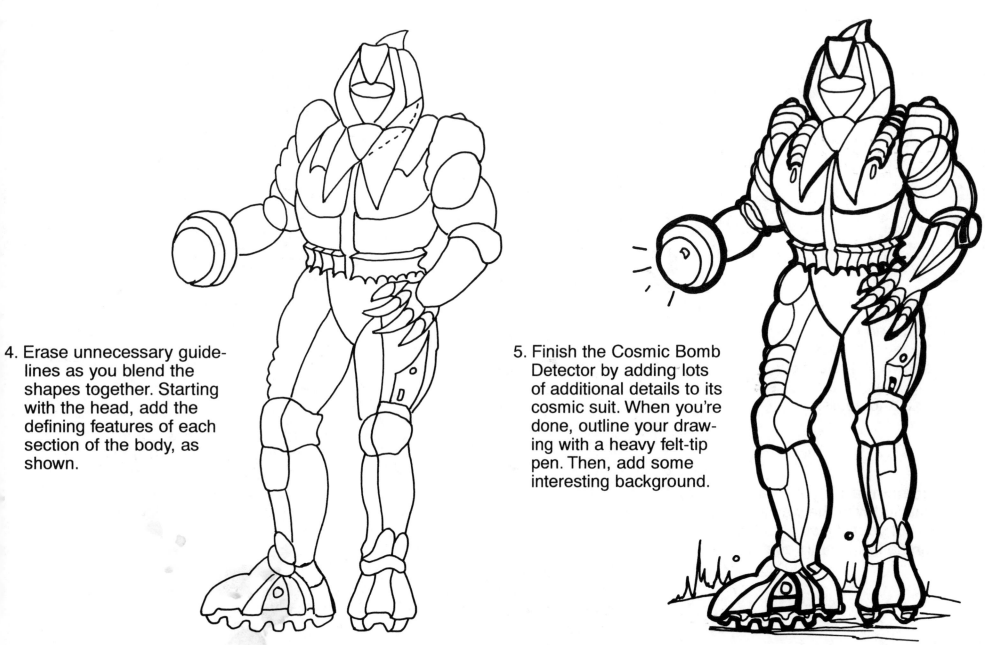

Hint: Keep erasing and drawing until you are satisfied with the way your alien looks.

4. Erase unnecessary guide-lines as you blend the shapes together. Starting with the head, add the defining features of each section of the body, as shown.

5. Finish the Cosmic Bomb Detector by adding lots of additional details to its cosmic suit. When you're done, outline your drawing with a heavy felt-tip pen. Then, add some interesting background.

COMMANDER GANTAR

1. Draw an oval for the head in the pose shown. Add the flowing lines for the neck and shoulders.

Remember: If you're not satisfied with the way any part of your drawing looks, erase it and start again.

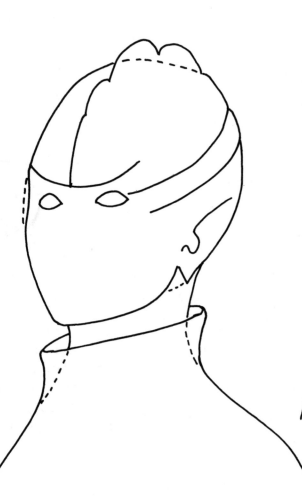

2. Add the uniform's collar. Then, add guidelines for the eyes, ear, and head features.

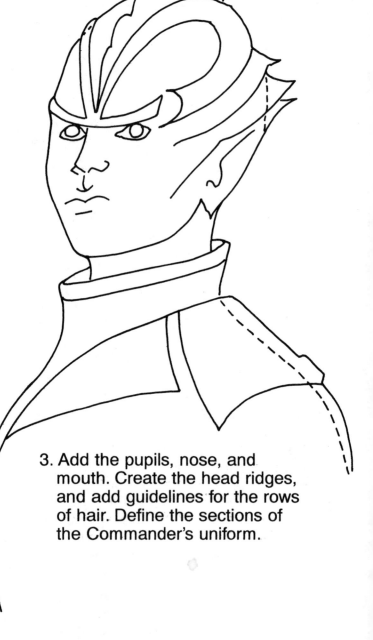

3. Add the pupils, nose, and mouth. Create the head ridges, and add guidelines for the rows of hair. Define the sections of the Commander's uniform.

4. Draw Gantar's hair and complete his facial features. Sketch in the other details to the face—the wavy lines on the bridge of the nose, and the markings on the chin and around the eyes. Start adding details to the uniform.

5. Add the remaining details. When you're finished, outline your drawing with a thick, felt-tip pen.

TITONIC, THE EVIL ALIEN

Note: This is one of the more difficult aliens to draw. But if you follow along carefully, step by step, you will be able to draw almost anything. It takes patience, practice, and lots of erasing to learn how to draw.

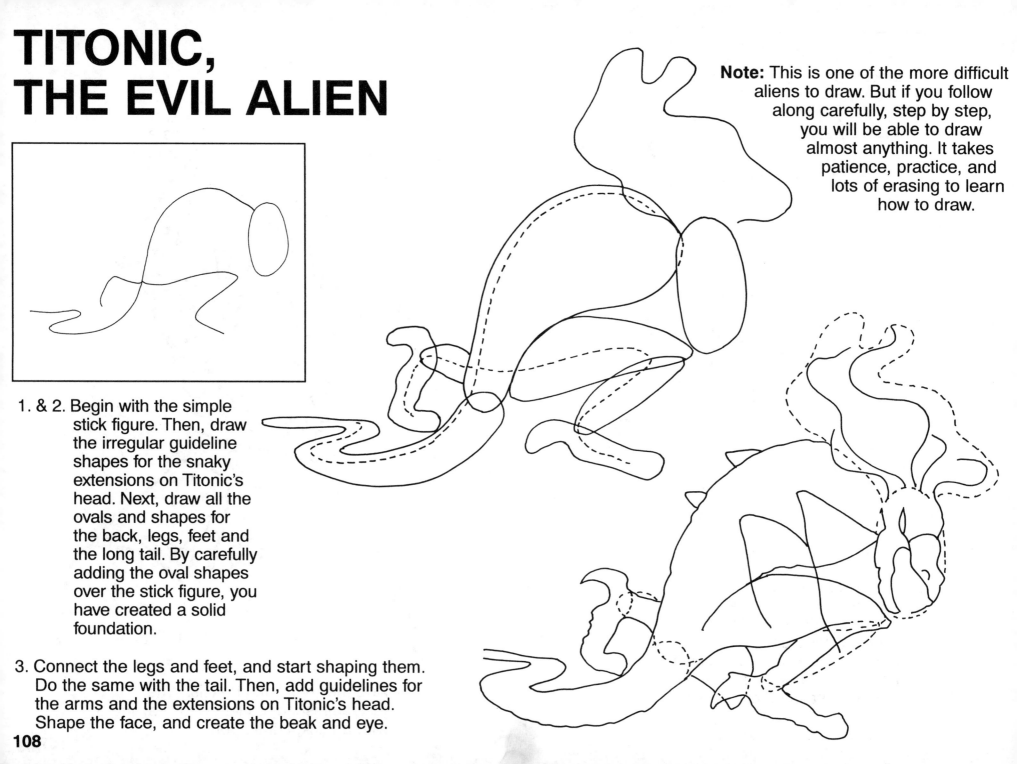

1. & 2. Begin with the simple stick figure. Then, draw the irregular guideline shapes for the snaky extensions on Titonic's head. Next, draw all the ovals and shapes for the back, legs, feet and the long tail. By carefully adding the oval shapes over the stick figure, you have created a solid foundation.

3. Connect the legs and feet, and start shaping them. Do the same with the tail. Then, add guidelines for the arms and the extensions on Titonic's head. Shape the face, and create the beak and eye.

5. For the finishing touches, add as many
wrinkles and spots to this alien's creepy
skin as you like. Then, draw a fiery floor
or another background for it to walk
through.

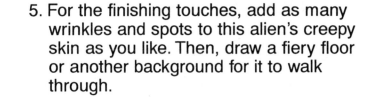

4. Continue working on the evil face until you're
satisfied with the way it looks. Draw lots of
long, curved, sharp teeth. Next, work on the
wavy, snakelike back of the head. Then,
carefully create the arms and hands. Don't
forget the tip of the tail.

STARDUST PARASITE

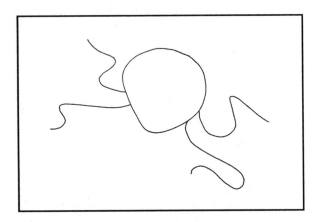

1. & 2. Start by drawing a large oval shape and four flowing lines. They can be flowing in any direction you wish. Add two more lines, and create four of the tentacles, as shown.

3. Create the other two tentacles. Start drawing the parts of the tentacles that wrap around the head, as shown. Keep erasing unneeded guidelines as you go along.

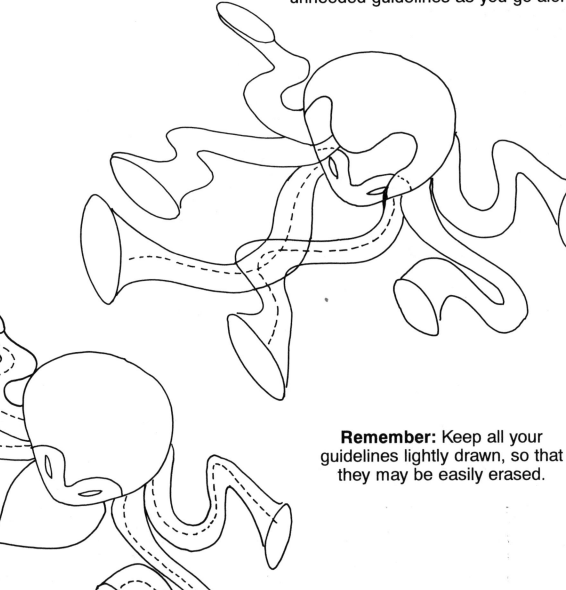

Remember: Keep all your guidelines lightly drawn, so that they may be easily erased.

4. Continue working on the tentacles wrapped around the head. Start drawing ovals on the inside of the tentacles' open ends. This will make them appear hollow. Lastly, begin adding the claws to several tentacles.

If you have had fun drawing these aliens, you may want to think of more to draw. Use the steps you have learned and create your own galactic aliens.

5. Add some details to the head and some star dust. The more star dust the parasite sucks in, the bigger its brain grows.

Hint: Don't be afraid to erase. It usually takes lots of drawing and erasing before you will be satisfied with the way this alien looks.

111

BULLZO

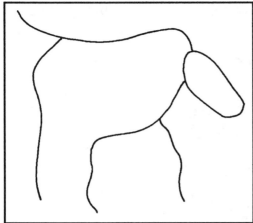

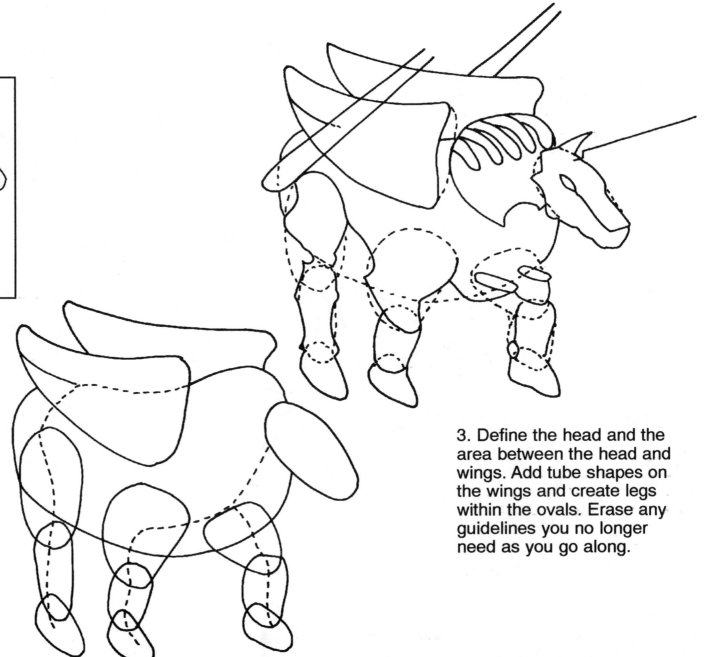

1. & 2.
Lightly sketch the stick figure. Then add guideline shapes for legs and wings, and draw the lower part of the body.

Note: This creature may seem more difficult to draw than most, but if you carefully work on one section at a time, you will soon be satisfied with your work.

3. Define the head and the area between the head and wings. Add tube shapes on the wings and create legs within the ovals. Erase any guidelines you no longer need as you go along.

5. Add as much detail as you want. When you're done, outline your drawing with a magic marker or felt-tip pen.

4. Start to refine each section of Bullzo's body. Begin at the head and work your way back to the wings. Then complete one leg at a time.

SNEAKEE

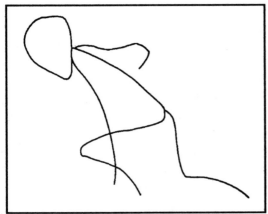

1. & 2. Draw a strawberry-shaped oval for the head and the basic stick figure. Carefully add the oval and the free-form guideline shapes for the rest of the figure.

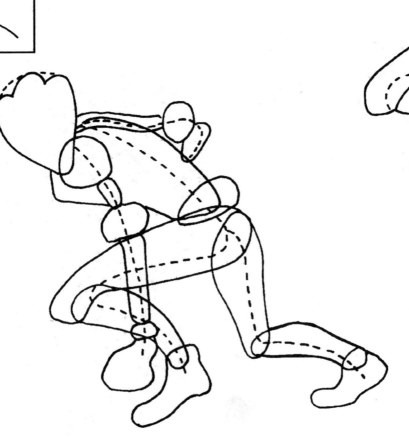

3. Sketch Sneakee's eyes and add five lines protruding from his head. Create fingers and combine the shapes, erasing unnecessary guidelines.

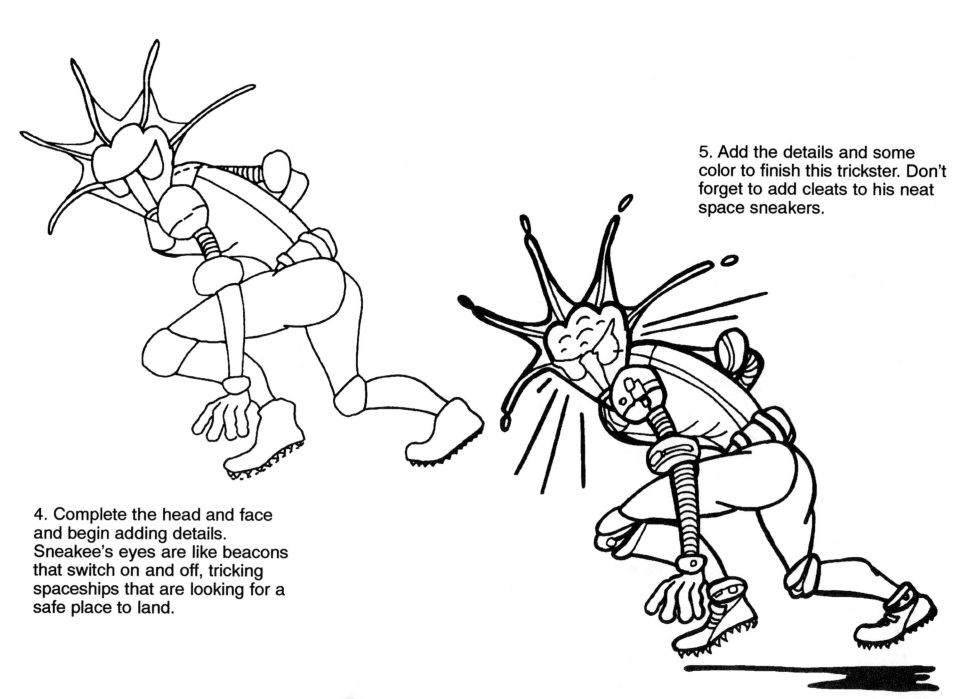

5. Add the details and some color to finish this trickster. Don't forget to add cleats to his neat space sneakers.

4. Complete the head and face and begin adding details. Sneakee's eyes are like beacons that switch on and off, tricking spaceships that are looking for a safe place to land.

AIRODAKTYL

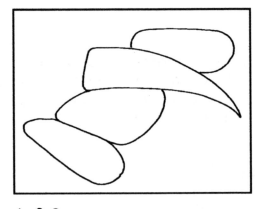

1. & 2.
Draw the four simple
shapes and the lines as
shown.

3. Carefully sketch wings
and a tail section. Go lightly
so that it will be easier to
erase unneeded guidelines.

Note: This UFO resembles
a bird and is a little more
complicated to draw. Go
slowly and try to see the
differences in each shape
and how they relate to
each other.

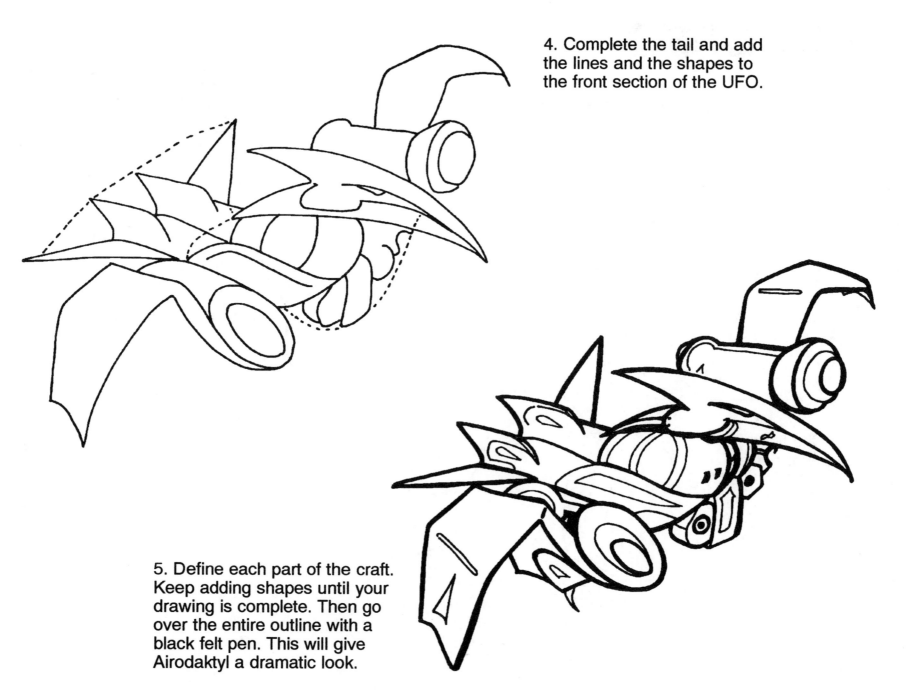

4. Complete the tail and add the lines and the shapes to the front section of the UFO.

5. Define each part of the craft. Keep adding shapes until your drawing is complete. Then go over the entire outline with a black felt pen. This will give Airodaktyl a dramatic look.

BUGG OFFO

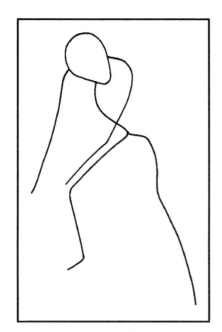

Note: It's easy to draw almost anything if you first build a good foundation.

1. & 2.
Draw the line figure starting with the oval head. Carefully add all the overlapping ovals. Draw the torso first, then add one limb at a time.

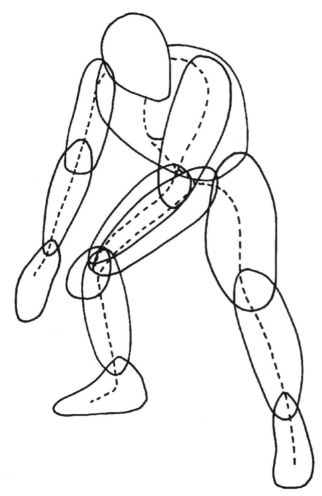

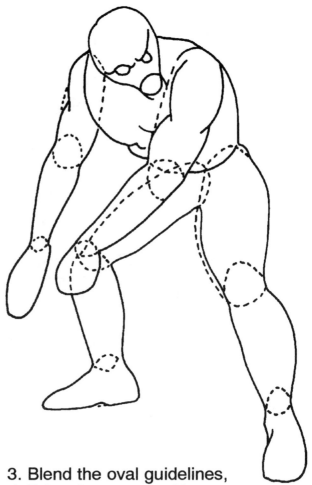

3. Blend the oval guidelines, defining the arms and legs. Start drawing facial features.

4. Bugg Offo is a mean-looking space pirate. Snaggle-tooth fangs help to give his face a menacing look. Define fingers and add gloves and boots. Add details to Bugg Offo's back.

5. Darken one of Bugg Offo's eyes and complete your details. When you're satisfied with your drawing, add mean colors for the finishing touches.

119

Here is an imaginary landscape of
a place that an alien or UFO might come
from. Use your imagination to create your
own landscape.

UFOs

Here are a few examples of UFOs.
Try drawing them, then use your imagination to create others.
You may want to add one or more as background to your alien drawings.

Use these pages to draw your own aliens and UFOs.